Choose Power

Power

Tools and Techniques for
Home and Work

First published by O Books, 2009
O Books is an imprint of John Hunt Publishing Ltd., The Bothy, Deershot Lodge, Park Lane, Ropley,
Hants, SO24 0BE, UK
office1@o-books.net
www.o-books.net

Distribution in:	South Africa
	Alternative Books
UK and Europe	altbook@peterhyde.co.za
Orca Book Services	Tel: 021 555 4027 Fax: 021 447 1430
orders@orcabookservices.co.uk	
Tel: 01202 665432 Fax: 01202 666219	Text copyright Pammyla Brooks 2008
Int. code (44)	
	Design: Stuart Davies
USA and Canada	
NBN	ISBN: 978 1 84694 170 2
custserv@nbnbooks.com	
Tel: 1 800 462 6420 Fax: 1 800 338 4550	All rights reserved. Except for brief quotations
	in critical articles or reviews, no part of this
	book may be reproduced in any manner without
Australia and New Zealand	prior written permission from the publishers.
Brumby Books	
sales@brumbybooks.com.au	
Tel: 61 3 9761 5535 Fax: 61 3 9761 7095	The rights of Pammyla Brooks as author have
	been asserted in accordance with the
Far East (offices in Singapore, Thailand,	Copyright, Designs and Patents Act 1988.
Hong Kong, Taiwan)	
Pansing Distribution Pte Ltd	
kemal@pansing.com	A CIP catalogue record for this book is available
Tel: 65 6319 9939 Fax: 65 6462 5761	from the British Library.

Printed by Digital Book Print

Choose Power

Tools and Techniques for Home and Work

Pammyla Brooks

BOOKS

Winchester, UK
Washington, USA

CONTENTS

List of Techniques

Acknowledgements

First, and foremost, all my thanks go to my partner, husband, and soul-mate, Mike Dooley. You give me the wings to fly free so that I can become who I was meant to be. I am grateful that I truly understand unconditional love, now, because you embody it daily as we share our life together.

Thanks to my mother, Jan Pogodzinski, who fostered my talents and continues to offer encouragement. Thank you for being a rock of strength for me.

My friend, Mary, shares incredible spiritual wisdom and insights that bring deeper meaning to my life.

I am very grateful to Linda Menchen, my very first reader, and a phenomenal and fantastic editor.

Thank you to the four of you for encouraging me from the beginning and throughout the completion of this book. I appreciate your strong editing skills and the many gifts you bring to my life.

In addition, I want to thank sister, Kim, for your loving support and for helping me through the darkest period of my life.

I express gratitude and love for the wonderful women I have met through RCGI, and my other supportive friends.

Finally, I appreciate Trish Rollins for her endless source of inspiration, optimism and support towards all of my endeavors.

Most of all, I thank you, the reader. I have written this book especially for you. I hope that this book contains what you need to design your dreams, and then to take pride in making them come true.

Introduction

"Power is the faculty or capacity to act,
The strength and potency to accomplish something.
It is the vital energy to make choices and decisions."
- Stephen Covey

This definition of Power comes from the book, *The Seven Habits of Highly Effective People: Powerful Lessons in Personal Change.*

What does Power mean to you?

Stop for a moment, right now, and think back to the last time when you remember feeling Powerful. It can be any time and any place.

Have you remembered a time?

Answer the following questions about your memory:

~ When you feel Powerful, what words best describe how you feel?
~ Where in your body do you feel Powerful?

Whenever I use the word Power in this book, remember this feeling and your answers to the questions. This internal Power is what I refer to throughout this book. Although Power might feel different from person to person, we all know when we feel Powerful and when we do not.

As the title of this book suggests, this feeling deep within ourselves is something that we can choose to feel at any time. This book contains the tools and techniques that remind us how to reconnect with our Power, even during challenging situations at work and at home.

Success Stories

> "What I do is based on powers we all have inside us;
> The ability to endure;
> The ability to love, to carry on,
> to make the best of what we have
> - And you don't have to be a 'Superman' to do it."
> - Christopher Reeve

Huge changes in your life are possible by using this book, and are only limited by your own personal intentions. Here are two examples of how this book can be used.

Peter was a new salesman. He practiced the conversational techniques provided in Chapter 2, so that he knew which words to use generously throughout his conversations, and which words to remove, since they break the connections between people. Since Peter also had problems sleeping, he experimented with the Calming Technique presented in Chapter 1. It did help him to sleep better, and then he started to feel the Blissful Moments described in the book.

Sandra was feeling overwhelmed by her life and often sank into periods of depression. She was feeling unappreciated at work, unlucky in love and she couldn't seem to control her three-year-old son. When she learned the Modified Extinction techniques from Chapter 2 and practiced them with her son, she noticed immediate results and realized how she was affecting his behavior. Empowered and encouraged, she used the Pacing and Leading technique from Chapter 2 to help her to successfully negotiate a raise with her boss.

After she taught herself how to use a pendulum, with the help of the techniques from Chapter 3, she learned that she needed to take B vitamins regularly. She used her pendulum to pick out the brand and dosage that was best for her, and she does not get migraine headaches at all anymore.

She was so encouraged with her results that she decided to tackle her "unlucky in love" issue. The Power of Attraction section opened her eyes to the pattern of men that she continued to attract into her life. She decided that the pattern started with her emotionally unavailable father, so she worked through the Forgiveness techniques in Chapter 6. Then, she created a Well-Formed Intention which listed the qualities that she wanted in her ideal man, as presented in Chapter 5. In less than 6 months, the man with all of the qualities walked into her life, and they are still together.

You can experience similar life-transforming results with this book, too. The following summary provides a taste of each chapter.

Chapter Summary

Chapter 1 contains techniques to help us feel more power and vitality in our bodies, minds and spirits.

Chapter 2 explains how to improve communication and power with people, and also how to set boundaries and end relationships when necessary.

Chapter 3 introduces a tool to work with the wisdom and Power of the Body.

Chapter 4 explores the Power of Attraction with regard to people we attract, information we attract and experiences we attract.

Chapter 5 builds on this by introducing the keys to successful Creative Visualizations that bring desired results into our lives.

Chapter 6 discusses the Power of the Mind and the Emotions. In addition to the Three Mind Keys, we learn about the power from memories.

Chapter 7 addresses Spiritual Power, and explains how love and gratitude can enhance our lives.

Have you ever used a recipe to make a tasty new meal? Following steps makes it easier to learn something new. That is

3

why this book provides the specific steps to follow so that each of the techniques is easy to learn. Although the techniques are not complex, they can transform your life.

The "recipes" in this book provide the keys to any results that you desire to have in your life. What do you want?

Here is a sample of questions that are answered in the pages that lie ahead:

~ How can I feel more power and vitality in my body right now?
~ How do I control my thoughts and emotions?
~ What are the best ways to improve communication with another person?
~ How do I effectively end a relationship with someone?
~ How can I get answers to questions I have about my health or other immediate concerns?
~ How do I take the "juice" out of a bad memory that is haunting me?
~ How do I attract more of what I really want into my life?
~ Which words sound like music to the ears and which words are best to avoid?

How to Use this Book

The step-by-step techniques or "recipes" can be done anywhere you are. Some of them take less than 20 seconds. Many incredible books would be more helpful if they offered practical ways to put their ideas into immediate action. Since this book provides the steps to follow, take advantage of this golden opportunity! Read the techniques, and then DO the techniques to truly experience the depth of your personal power.

Choose Power right here, right now. Wherever you are reading this book is a good place to do a technique, since many of them are quick. Keep a journal or a notebook nearby to record your journey. Readers have worked through my techniques like a seminar-in-a-book.

Anyone can benefit from these techniques. Christians, Jews, Muslims, Buddhists and those who follow the Goddess can tailor the techniques so that they work better with individual beliefs and values.

Add specific details that will make the techniques more fun and playful, or more sacred and spiritual, depending on the technique. For example, you might say your favorite prayers, or hold your hands a certain way, or use your own pictures or personal items.

Those of you who prefer to jump around in a book will enjoy this book as much as those who read the book cover to cover. There are options at the end of certain techniques to jump to other sections. Watch for **Suggestions** that point out other sections to visit. The Selected Index at the back of the book can quickly deliver a page number for any of the terms or techniques in the book.

I am interested in reading and hearing your stories and feedback after you have used the techniques in this book. I am also interested in any new ideas. What do you do to feel more powerful at home or at work? Maybe you have a personal tool or technique that you would like to share with me. Tell me about it at my website: Pammyla@Pammyla.com. You can also find out information about my upcoming speaking engagements, weekend workshops or online classes.

Now, without further delay, let us begin to practice the keys to feeling more powerful in our lives. We can feel good in body, mind and spirit and enjoy our lives more often and more fully by Choosing Power.

Questions Answered in Chapters

How do I feel more powerful right now?
Chapter 1: Feel Your Power

Which words sound like music to the ears and which words are best to avoid?
Chapter 2: Power with People

How do I effectively end relationships with certain people?
Chapter 2: Power with People

How do I find out specific answers about what is best for me right now?
Chapter 3: Power of the Body

Why do I keep attracting the same kind of partner?
Or job situation?
Or life event?
Chapter 4: Power of Attraction

How do I get what I specifically want in my life?
Chapter 5: Power of Intention

How can I control my thoughts and emotions?
Chapter 6: Power of the Mind and the Emotions

How can love and gratitude help my life?
Chapter 7: Spiritual Power

CHAPTER 1

Feeling Powerful

"You have no power over me."
- *The Labyrinth (1986)*

These are the magic words that free the heroine from danger and return her to safety at the end of the movie. She suddenly remembers that the scary demon, played by David Bowie, has no power over her. She realizes that she can save herself, and suddenly she is safe.

When Jaclyn first picked up this book she didn't know what Power meant. All she knew was when she felt good and when she felt bad. She felt good when she was around her friends and she usually felt bad around her boss at work.

She practiced the techniques in this chapter and discovered that the techniques did help her to feel good. She felt more confident, and decided to test out some of the Conversational Techniques from Chapter 2 with her boss. These techniques worked for her and so she also felt more powerful at work.

The tools and techniques in this book remind us that the words above are true for us, too. Nothing else has power over us. If other people, stressful events, bad feelings or something else produced previous feelings of powerlessness, now we can use this book to feel the strength and joy resulting from Choosing Power with people, from our bodies, with our minds and emotions and more.

We know when we are feeling powerful. In contrast, when we feel physically drained or mentally tired or spiritually empty, we can feel overwhelmed by our lives and powerless. It is hard to deal with other people, or work with our minds and emotions, if we do not feel good.

We all feel tired or run down from time to time. Perhaps we exerted a lot of energy at work or with our children. Maybe we didn't get enough sleep the night before. We each find our own favorite ways to feel good. What do you do? I love espresso in an Americano. Many of us use caffeine and sugar for a quick "pick-me-up." Since this is a short-term fix, we often feel more drained of energy and power when it wears off.

There are other alternatives that we can choose. This first chapter provides ways to feel more power in our bodies, minds and spirits whenever we choose.

First, the Calming Technique is presented. The second technique can increase our power in less than 20 seconds. Then, we will increase our power from water. Finally, we will create personalized lists of the people, places and events that increase our feelings of power.

The Calming Technique

Calming ourselves is a great first step to increase our power. Once we are calm, then we can better access the power in our minds, bodies, and spirits that is just waiting to be awakened and used to our benefit.

You may already have done something similar before. Perhaps you do relaxation techniques or say prayers or simply allow yourself to be still and relax. This technique is not very different from these examples, and it is very simple.

The Calming Technique can help us to feel relaxed in our bodies, a sense of peace in our minds and in control of our emotions. I have noticed that I do not seem to get as angry as I did before I began to do this technique regularly. Instead of feeling overpowered by my temper, I now have more control. For example, now if something happens, I realize that I have a choice. I can choose to either get upset, or to let it go and not get upset.

The Calming Technique has become such an important part of

my life that I tend to have problems sleeping now whenever I have skipped my evening session. Practice it now because the Calming Technique is an important step in many of the techniques in the book.

Technique 1 – Calming Technique

Purpose: To learn a technique to increase your power.

This first step in many of the techniques in this book helps us to relax the mind, body, and spirit. It can last any length of time, from two or three minutes to much longer.

It is better to sit up than to lie down so that you do not fall asleep. You may prefer to lean against a wall or a couch, or to sit on a chair. If you are unable to sit and must lie down, then keep your arms bent so the elbows are at 90-degree angles. That way, if you do fall asleep, your hands will fall onto you and wake you up.

Choose a comfortable place that you can use over and over again for this purpose, if possible. Once the mind and body learn to get into a calm state in one certain location, simply being in that same location can bring on the calm state.

1) Choose a quiet space, where there will be no distractions from people, pets, the telephone, the television or anything else.

2) Sit comfortably, as described above.

3) Close your eyes. Breathe slowly and deeply. Concentrate on each breath in and each breath out.

4) Allow your mind to clear by letting go of all thoughts, concerns and worries. The key is to allow rather than to force. Your brain is used to thinking, so thoughts may come

back into your mind.

Allow your mind to be like a river, carrying leaves and sticks through its waters as it flows past you. Just as you might notice a stick float by, you might notice yourself thinking about your job, a friend or a family member.

As soon as you realize you are thinking about something, let the thought go. Watch it travel down the river away from you.

Continue to notice what is occurring in your mind, and continue to remind yourself to clear your mind and let thoughts go. Whenever you remember to do this is the right time to do it.

The mind may begin to think a thought the first time you do this, and perhaps each and every time that you do the Calming Technique. That is normal. Simply let the thought go when you notice that your mind has grasped on to something. The mind is used to thinking and so it takes some time for it to learn that it is safe to stop thinking. Although you may not do it perfectly the first time, failure is impossible. The mind becomes easier to clear with practice.

Set special time aside just for this. For the best success, treat the Calming Technique like a gift that you give to yourself rather than something that you "have to do." You will find that it IS a tremendous gift to give your mind and body a break from the everyday stress of life.

For the purpose of the techniques in this book, do the Calming Technique until you feel calm. You might find yourself doing this technique for longer periods of time because it is so relaxing. Although I enjoy 20 and 30 minute sessions, I also notice powerful effects when I only do it for 5 minutes.

The Calming Technique is an example of meditation. Someone once told me that, "prayer is when we talk to God, and meditation is when God talks to us." Meditation quiets the mind so that we can listen.

Studies have shown that numerous mental, emotional and physical health benefits result from meditating on a regular basis. It has helped to reduce stress, depression and pain. Because we learn to calm ourselves whenever we want, it can help to decrease high blood pressure and anxiety.

Once we learn how to clear our minds whenever we choose, we can stop the thoughts that may run around our heads at night and keep us awake. We can also experience a sense of peace from practicing meditation on a regular basis. This sense of peace occurs at other times, even when we are not meditating. Other benefits of the Calming Technique and meditation include the Blissful Moments and Sudden Insights, which are explained in the next sections.

Can you feel effortless as you do the Calming Technique instead of fighting the mind? It is the opposite of "doing" or "trying." Have you ever had the experience of being unable to remember someone's name, and the more you work at it, the more elusive the name is? The name only pops in our minds when we stop "trying" and think about something else. Similarly, Blissful Moments occur when we stop fighting the mind.

Blissful Moments
While doing the Calming Technique, I love the feelings of complete joy that I have experienced. Simply taking the time to stop and center myself allows them to occur. Blissful Moments may range from less than a minute to 30 minutes or more. I call them "moments" because they occur during times when I am completely in the present, in the here and now, and so I am not sure how long the moments have lasted. Some of them seem to last pretty long.

During these Blissful Moments, I am not thinking about the past; I am not worrying about the future. Blissful Moments occur when I have been successful at clearing my mind for a short period of time.

The bliss is spiritual, emotional and physical. In addition to feeling emotionally joyful and spiritually connected, I experience physical sensations of bliss at the top of my head. It feels like parts of my brain are glowing and tingling.

When I feel the bliss, if I start to feel proud of myself or attempt to prolong the blissful feeling, it will vanish. On the other hand, smiling and enjoying the feeling allows it to continue. Again, the Blissful Moments occur during times when I have successfully stopped the thoughts so that I am free to enjoy the moment.

Here is a picture that might help. Think about our brains as two mirrors facing each other. When a thought occurs, the brain uses these mirrors to look at it from different perspectives.

When there are no thoughts in that space between the mirrors, they are simply reflecting each other and bliss occurs. As soon as a thought starts running through the brain and between the mirrors, the stillness is broken and the bliss stops.

The Blissful Moments may be elusive; however, the more that you practice the technique, the more likely it will be that you will experience them. Those feelings of ecstasy are one reason that I continue to meditate. Sudden Insights that pop in my head are another reason.

Sudden Insights

When we learn to quiet the chatter that goes on in the mind using the Calming Technique or meditation, then there is a chance to listen and learn. I am amazed at the insights that I have received when I have successfully cleared my mind.

I have learned about myself, and had great insights about my health, friends and co-workers. I have been inspired with great ideas, and developed some of the techniques in this book.

Salvador Dali, Albert Einstein and Thomas Edison practiced various forms of meditation and experienced these sudden insights, too, and so can you.

> "The intellect has little to do on the road to discovery.
> There comes a leap in consciousness,
> call it intuition or what you will,
> and the solution comes to you
> and you don't know how or why."
> - Albert Einstein

The Calming Technique is one great way to unleash the vitality and power in our minds, bodies and spirits. Please see the Meditation Basics section in Appendix A if you would like more information. The rest of this chapter explores other ways to unlock the vitality in our bodies.

Increasing Vitality in the Body

Our bodies hold a lot of power. Let's unlock that power to make it work for us in our lives. First, we will learn two new techniques. Later in the chapter we will identify the specific people, places and activities that make us feel good and increase our power.

I call this first technique the Power Pose. Use this technique any time when you need a quick burst of power and vitality. This might be done at the beginning of your day to feel energized or after a long, tiring day. The best part is that it takes less than one minute. The Power Pose is the quickest and easiest way to get a power boost.

Technique 2 - The Power Pose

Purpose: To learn a technique that will increase your feelings of energy and power in about 20 seconds.

When you do this technique for the first couple of times, hold the pose only for the amount of time that it takes to slowly inhale and exhale three breaths (20 seconds).

Power Pose steps:
1) Sit or stand. If you stand, spread your legs as far apart as your shoulders. As shown in the picture, hold your arms out to the sides of you and bend them so that each arm forms the letter V with your elbow at the bottom edge.

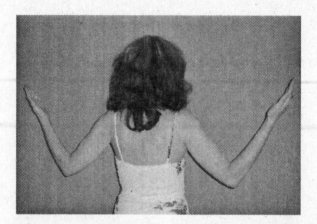

Keep your arms like this throughout the technique.
2) Breathe slowly and deeply. Keep your mind on your breathing. Concentrate on drawing complete breaths into your body. Many times, especially during stressful situations, we stop breathing or we breathe shallowly. When you breathe in, feel your stomach getting bigger.

When you exhale, feel your stomach get flat again. It is important to work the stomach like this while breathing.

3) As you stand in the Power Pose, close your eyes, quiet your mind and connect with your spirit. Here are some recommendations for connecting with your spirit. Choose one that might work well with your background and experiences. As with every technique, tailor it for yourself.

   ~ Use the Calming technique described earlier in this chapter to get into a relaxed or calm state.

   ~ Say a favorite prayer.

   ~ Meditate using a mantra from Appendix A, if you choose.

   ~ Express gratitude for the blessings in your life.

   ~ Imagine that you are a tree and feel your roots moving deep into the earth bringing nutrients and energy up into your body.

   ~ Concentrate on absorbing the healing energy that surrounds you.

4) Feel your Power. Imagine yourself pulling energy into your body and that it is going where it is most needed. Perhaps you have a sore back, or you want to focus energy on your heart or another part of your body that needs healing. Feel the energy where needed in your body, or throughout your body.

5) When you are finished, open your eyes, let your arms relax and enjoy your additional energy and feelings of power.

After you have done the Power Pose a couple of times, you may increase it to a full 60 seconds. How does that feel for you? After that, follow your own intuition about the length of time to do it.

You might experiment with the placement of your arms until it feels right to you. Some folks may feel more comfortable with arms being bent in a **V** position as described, while others may prefer for their arms to be straighter. Do what feels right to you. Everyone is different. In addition, some days the arms might prefer to be in a different position than other days. It is fine to open or close your hands or let them twist if they want to. Follow your intuition and listen to your body because they know what is best for you.

As you continue to practice this technique, monitor how you feel. How does your energy level compare to when you started? Do you feel more powerful or less powerful than when you started?

Done correctly, the Power Pose increases your energy and personal power. If you feel more drained, and less energetic after you do it, or if your arms get noticeably tired, then you are doing it too long. Continue to modify the technique so that it successfully increases your energy and power.

Now you have a technique that you can do in less than a minute whenever you need a quick power boost at home or at work. When I used to teach this technique in my Public Speaking classes, I explained how this could be done in the bathroom shortly before speaking in front of a group. You will likely come up with other great uses for this technique.

As noted above, in addition to being effective, this technique is quick. The next technique also increases your vitality, and requires about 20 minutes.

Power from Water

Another way to restore energy and power in our bodies is with water. An adult body is made up of 70 per cent water, so it makes sense that water can help us feel restored. We use water to restore our power in so many ways. Swimming, listening to bubbling brooks and watching waves break against the shore are a few examples.

The following technique is another way to use water to help restore emotional, physical and mental power. I have successfully used this technique to improve bad menstrual cramps, sore muscles from working out and even hangovers.

Technique 3 – The Power Bath

Purpose: To increase your power and energy using water.

1) Fill a bathtub with water at a temperature that is comfortable to you.
2) Add Epsom salts and Baking Soda in a ratio of 2:1. For example, 2 small cups of Epsom salts with 1 small cup of Baking Soda works well in a typical bathtub. However, you may experiment with more or less, using the same ratios.
3) Light candles, play your favorite music or do whatever else makes you feel nurtured. If reading a good book or eating chocolate makes you feel good, then do that. You might also want to turn off the telephone and anything else that might disturb you.
4) Soak in the bathtub for at least 20 minutes to get the maximum benefit.
5) When you get out, notice how your body and soul feel energized. Compare your energy level to how you felt beforehand.

Epsom salt baths are widely known for their effective relief of body pain such as from injuries, working out, arthritis, and menstrual cramps. When the Epsom salts are combined with the baking soda in bath water, the effect is like "cleaning the aura," as one doctor described it. In addition to feeling physically energized and more powerful, you will notice an increase in emotional and mental power.

Another reason why this may be so effective is that the Power Bath is a great gift to give to ourselves. Our bodies feel our love and gratitude and are immediately recharged.

All people can feel recharged from the Power Pose and the Power Bath. Because not all people are restored by the Power from Fire, Appendix B contains information and techniques for restoring your power using fire.

The next section helps us to remember the people, places and activities that help us to feel more powerful. We will each create our own personal Power Lists.

Creating Power Lists

Think about the people, places and activities that make you feel good. Certain physical, mental, emotional and spiritual activities can all increase our sense of power.

Who or what makes you feel powerful? How do you get energized?

Which people make you feel good? Who makes you laugh? These are good people to spend time with.

Extroverts tend to feel more energized by being around a lot of people, at parties and other similar events. Introverts tend to feel more powerful by spending time alone, or with one or two close friends instead of a large group. What do you prefer?

Think about your personal power places. Where do you go to feel good? Do you often find yourself unwinding by walking, hiking or swimming in nature? Places like this help to connect us back to our power. What other places help you feel more powerful?

How do you like to experience the power in your body? Any time that we use our bodies in a physical activity, we can feel our personal power. Do you enjoy running, swimming or lifting weights? Do you like to walk, dance, do Tai Chi, yoga or martial arts? Karate and judo help many people to feel more powerful. Some people like to work in gardens to get re-energized. Kissing and other affectionate activities with a loved one is another great way to feel powerful in the body.

What mental, emotional and spiritual activities give you energy? Do you like talking on the phone for hours? Is reading a good book more your style? Does painting or embroidery or a similar creative activity put you in touch with your power? Do you participate in online groups, games, or other similar activities?

It is important to know who and what increases your experience of power. Use these questions and the next checklist to help you to recall and identify specific people, places and events that consistently help you to feel more powerful. This list will come in handy when we are practicing Immediate Distraction and some of the other techniques in this book.

Technique 4 – Power Lists

Purpose: To make a list of people, places and activities
that increase personal power.

On the following checklist, mark the boxes in front of the
items that help you feel more powerful. Ignore the items
that make you feel less powerful or that rate as neutral to
you. Do not feel that you have to mark your spouse or your
children because you should. Only mark the ones that truly
make you feel more powerful or energized than you were
before. No one has to see this list except for you.

There are no right or wrong answers since everyone is
different. If you are not sure whether an item on the list
increases your personal power or not, test it out and check
whether it empowers you.

People who make me feel powerful

☐ My children
☐ My spouse or significant other
☐ Particular friend(s) or family member(s): _____

_____

☐ Specific groups: _____

_____

☐ Other: _____

Places that make me feel powerful

☐ Being home alone
☐ Connecting with nature in these places: _____

_____

☐ Going to a movie
☐ Going to a library
☐ Worshipping together with a group on Sunday
☐ Going to these places: _____
_____

Events and Activities that make me feel powerful

☐ Going to Parties
☐ Running
☐ Hiking
☐ Walking
☐ Swimming
☐ Dancing
☐ Singing
☐ Playing music
☐ Judo, Karate, Tae Kwon Do
☐ Doing Pilates
☐ Working Out
☐ Talking on the phone
☐ Calming Technique
☐ Meditating
☐ Cooking
☐ Reading
☐ Taking a (Power) bath
☐ Creative activities like artwork
☐ Doing housework
☐ Online activities
☐ Pets or other animals
☐ Kissing and other intimate activities
☐ Yoga
☐ Gardening
☐ My favorite hobbies: _____
☐ Other: _____
☐ Other: _____
☐ Other: _____
☐ Other: _____

Perhaps you thought of some other ways that are not listed. Make sure to add them to your list, along with any others that occur to you while reading this book and living your life.

Now that you know what specific persons, places and

events help you to feel more powerful, you know exactly who to see, where to go and what to do when you are feeling run down.

Perhaps you have identified persons, places or events that drain your energy and power. Of course, it is best to avoid those, if possible, although many of us cannot avoid work or certain people indefinitely!

Check in with yourself often to see, hear and feel how you are doing. Stressful life events occur regularly. Choose Power by doing something on your Power List whenever you feel stressed or powerless. We will also use this list after certain other techniques in the book.

This chapter has explained several techniques that can be done in the privacy of your own home to increase feelings of power, such as the Calming Technique, the Power Pose, the Power Bath and items on your Power List. Take a moment every day to feel Powerful.

There are also things that you can do (and avoid doing) that will increase your power with people. The next chapter provides techniques for improving communication with people at home and at work, and also other techniques for setting boundaries and ending relationships.

CHAPTER 2

Power with People

"Our ultimate freedom
is the right and power to decide
how anybody or anything
outside ourselves
will affect us."
- Stephen Covey

One man who I would see at almost every party had a bad habit of saying very crude remarks to me. I asked him to stop saying disgusting things to me (which is an example of creating effective boundaries discussed later in this chapter). However, this man ignored my request, and continued to make rude sexual comments to me, so I used Modified Extinction (described towards the end of this chapter) with him.

As a result, he completely stopped. Now, I can chat with him at parties without having to endure his inappropriate sexual comments, although I suspect that he still makes them to other women. He probably does not even realize what I did or that he acts differently with me.

This chapter addresses how to increase our power with people who we encounter in our personal or professional lives. We begin with techniques to improve communication with people. Some of the techniques work well for conveying difficult information, or negotiating with someone or convincing someone to see your point of view.

After that, the chapter shifts to focus on effective ways to put boundaries in place with people or to change the nature of a relationship. The Effective Boundaries section can assist you with ideas to change the rules that operate in a certain relationship.

If you experiment with those techniques and the relationship continues to be a source of stress for you, you might decide to end the relationship completely. Although this may not be something you have done before, it is important to remember that it is an option at all times. The Power of No Attention (or Extinction) section completes the chapter and explains the most effective way to end a relationship with someone.

Conversational Techniques

This first section focuses on improving communication between people. Pacing and Leading is presented first. It is a technique that helps people to feel more at ease with each other.

Pacing and Leading

This technique works well in any conversation to communicate difficult information to someone. With practice, it can be useful in negotiations or disagreements. This two-step technique is called Pacing and Leading because first we Pace the other person's perspective, and then we Lead them to our perspective.

In the Pacing step, we begin by saying two or three sentences that are positive about the other person, or that review or summarize what the other person has already said. Think about how that person sees things, and the words he or she has used in the past to design the Pacing statements. When the other person feels understood and heard, then he or she will be more likely to be open to your information.

Next, in the Leading step, we state our opinion or the difficult information that we want to present. It is important to present the information in an objective manner. Simply state the facts or your opinion without blaming or criticizing the other person.

Here is an example. If I disagree with what another person has said, a Pacing and Leading response might be, "It sounds like you have really put some time and energy into preparing your idea. I appreciate you sharing that. Here is another idea."

I used this technique with a former supervisor to let her know that she hurt my feelings every time she made fun of me for not eating cake, cookies and other sweets with the rest of my co-workers. I said, "I know that you have a great sense of humor and like to make people laugh. I really like that about you. At the same time, when you make fun of me in front of the group, it really hurts my feelings and makes me not want to have lunch with the group." She responded well and said she wished I had told her sooner.

One reason that this technique works so well is that it makes us plan what we are going to say. We can pick the right words in advance, instead of taking a chance and saying the wrong thing at the wrong time. The next technique will walk us through the steps of planning what to say.

Technique 1 – Practice Pacing and Leading

Purpose: To practice a fantastic way to communicate difficult information to another person.

To practice Pacing and Leading, think of something difficult that you want to communicate to a friend or family member. Steps 1 - 5 will be done by yourself in preparation for the conversation you will have with the other person in Step 6. We will prepare the Leading statements first, and the Pacing statements second, which is backwards from how you will say it to the other person.

The first time, it is probably best to pick something with

"low stakes" to practice with, such as deciding where to go for dinner, rather than something with "high stakes," like asking for a raise. Once you have practiced this technique successfully with a friend or loved one, then you will feel more confident using this technique for more important matters, such as negotiating salary with your supervisor.

1) Get into a relaxed state using the Calming Technique described in the first chapter.
2) Prepare the Leading statements. Think about what difficult information you want to communicate. This will be used in the Leading step. Write down a couple of sentences that express your thoughts. Avoid blaming or criticizing the other person for anything. It is important that the other person does not feel threatened by your statements.
3) Prepare the Pacing statements. Brainstorm and write out statements that you can say that will accomplish one or more of the following purposes:
   ~ Make the other person feel valued.
   ~ Use words, phrases or ideas that the other person has said.
   ~ Summarize what the other person has said.

   Choose two or three sentences that flow together well. These are the Pacing statements.
4) Place the Pacing statements **before** the Leading statements created in Step 2. Read them together and modify the statements, if needed, so that they flow together well.
5) Practice. When you are still alone, say the entire one-sided conversation with your Pacing and Leading

statements out loud to yourself to hear how it sounds. Edit and revise as necessary so that the statements express your truth in a way that the other person can hear it without feeling defensive. Remember to avoid accusations.

6) When you are ready and when you feel that the timing is right, say it to the other person.

How did it work? What could you have done better?

Words that Sound Like Music to the Ears

Words that we use with ourselves and with others on a daily basis have power. What if every statement that we make, positive or negative, sends out an intention into the world?

The chapters on the Power of Attraction and the Power of Intention will take this idea further. For now, it is important to realize that words have power.

The next three sections discuss the words that we use in conversations. We begin with words that sound like music to the ears, continue with words to avoid, and end with words to buy time. These sections are not meant to be comprehensive. Use them as examples of the power of words as you listen to those you say and hear in conversations.

"I Agree"

In conversations in which we are in conflict with another person, it is easy to focus on the differences between what each person wants or values. It may be more difficult to find the areas and ideas that both people have in common. These are not usually included in discussions. However, even when two people disagree, areas of agreement still exist.

27

It is extremely helpful to do the extra work to find the common ground. When you are in negotiation with people, emphasize one or more areas upon which you agree. Then, you can use these words, "I agree," with honesty in your conversation, and they will sound like music to the other person's ears.

I know this to be true, because my partner often says these words to me. I love to hear them. It feels very good, and it often does not really matter what he says after that. In other words, it seems more important that he shares my opinion than what he thinks I am right about. Those words are often enough to turn my feelings around completely if we are in disagreement. If I am venting about someone or something, it makes me feel like he heard me.

In any case, using these words will definitely make another person feel good when you use them in your conversations. This might help you to come to an agreement, where there had only been disagreement before.

"You're Right"

Everyone loves to hear that they are right. We all have a secret desire to hear these words from other people.

As mentioned above, it is easy to identify differences between people when we are in conflict or negotiation. Although it is more challenging, listen closely to the other person to find something said that you think is correct. Harmony and agreements are more likely to occur when we identify similarities and focus on what we have in common.

You will be amazed, both by the power you feel from using these words, and from the way the conversation may turn after you use them. If the conversation is becoming tense, these words will cause the other person to soften up a bit. As you focus on the statement in which the other person was "right," he or she has a chance to feel powerful.

While in conflict with someone, finding something that he or she said that is "right" may not be easy. In addition, it might be difficult to admit in public that the other person is right (or that we are wrong) about something. Perhaps you remember the television series, "Happy Days." The Fonz was unable to say the words, "I'm wrong." They came out sounding like something else because he could not say them correctly.

If you are not familiar with this character, perhaps you know people like Fonzie who cannot admit that they are wrong. These people may also have a hard time saying "You're Right," to someone else because they think that they will lose power. However, the first time that they use the words, they will feel the power that comes from giving this gift to another person.

These are two examples of words to sprinkle into your conversations because people love to hear them. These words can also be used in the Pacing step while Pacing and Leading. You may think of other words along the same line.

As long as you are emphasizing what you both have in common, and focusing on the positive, the right words can help to bring about agreements and understanding between people with different points of view and different perspectives.

Avoid these Words

In addition to words that can produce better results in conversations, other words have the power to destroy the good feelings that occur between people.

Once you have spent time and energy creating good feelings and experiences between people, avoid using words that can destroy what has been built.

"But"

The word "but" can cause problems when we want to connect and communicate with people because it stops the good feelings that have been developing between us. In any sentence that uses the word, the section that comes after the word "but" becomes more important and is highlighted in the foreground, while the words that came before the "but" become less important and fade into the background. It can easily feel like a slap in the face, as you know if you have heard someone tell you, "I love you, but…"

If someone has said this to you, then you know that it is not a pleasant feeling. In this example, the "but" feels like it totally contradicts the phrase at the beginning. It minimizes the importance of the first part and draws attention to the second part.

Here is another example. A supervisor might say to an employee, "You have a great way with people, but you make too many mistakes." Again, the emphasis feels like it is on the mistakes. It would be better for the supervisor to rephrase the statement to say, "You have a great way with people, AND you would be more successful if you concentrated on making fewer mistakes in your work." Notice that when the supervisor takes the time to use "and" instead of "but," other words in the sentence naturally change, too, and so the tone sounds less like an accusation. In this example, the employee can take pride in the compliment because the sentence no longer emphasizes the mistakes.

To replace the word "but" in your speech, use "and" or "and at the same time." It may seem like a very small change to replace the word in your conversations. However, it feels very different on the receiving end of these statements.

In your everyday conversations, listen when other people use the word "but." Then, you will understand how much impact this little word can have.

Advanced Uses of "But"

Of course, it is not the word itself that is bad; it is the way that it is positioned in a sentence that leaves people with a bad feeling. It is important to repeat that using the word "but" puts the power on the words that come after it. Therefore, if the compliment comes before the word, using "but" will minimize the good feeling from the compliment and emphasize whatever is said after the word.

With that in mind, move the compliment so it comes after the word. Using the example above, it becomes, "I wish you would make fewer mistakes in your work, but you have such a great way with people." Notice how rearranging the words completely changes the way that the employee hears the sentence.

Once you understand the power in the positions of the phrases, then you can play with the word "but" and use it to add power to your conversations. For example, if you need to turn down an invitation, the word will add power when you say "I'm so sorry I can't make it, BUT please keep me in mind for the next time."

Understand the difference? It might take some practice to understand and use the word effectively. If it is still unclear, it might be simpler to completely remove the word from your vocabulary.

"Always" and "Never"

The use of these words can be deadly when used in a statement that sounds like an accusation. For example, "You never bring me flowers," or "You always forget to put the toilet seat up/down," are rarely true statements. Since an exception usually exists for every statement containing "always" or "never," it tends to put folks on the defensive when they hear it. Instead of focusing on the real issue, the other person will spend time and energy remembering the one time that the statement was not true, and now the conversation has turned into an argument.

For example, if I say to a friend, "You never come to my dinner parties," she will immediately remember the one party that she did attend and will bring that up. In this example, we will spend our time and energy arguing about my statement because what I said was really not true.

It is better for me to stop and think about what I really want to get across to my friend. Removing "always" and "never" from my sentences will force me to rethink what the actual message is that I want to convey. What is my true concern?

I could replace the statement with one that is more accurate and conveys my true message such as, "It hurts my feelings when you don't come to my dinner parties." Now, we can discuss the true concern, instead of wasting time and energy in an argument that will not solve the problem.

Avoiding the use of the words "always" and "never" will result in added honesty in our statements and conversations. Focus on conveying the actual truth and intent in statements, without using exaggerations. As a result, other people will be less likely to feel defensive and more likely to hear the true concern.

"Should" "Must" "Have To" "Required"

These words can feel harsh and offensive because they sound as if one person knows what is best for another person. It is as if the person is taking your power to choose away by telling you what to do. Whether you hear this word from your significant other, or a friend or someone else, notice how it immediately puts you on the defensive.

Some of us use these words on ourselves, too. Maybe we are using the words to convince ourselves to do something that we do not want to do. Perhaps we are holding ourselves up to some unrealistic standard.

The words are not effective because they do not let us ask whether it is an unrealistic standard or not. The words can immediately cause us to feel guilty for something that we did or did not do. In any case, using these words on ourselves is a sure way to increase the amount of stress we are experiencing, and to reduce our feelings of power.

My mother uses the saying, "Thou shalt not SHOULD on thyself or others." She remembers it when she finds herself using the word, and she says that it helps her to remember to avoid using the word with herself and others.

Replace these words in your conversations by softening your statements or asking questions, such as, "Maybe you want to think about," or "Have you considered...?"

A good question in response to any one of these words is, "What would happen if I didn't?" It is a good test because if there is not a good answer, then the power of the words vanishes immediately.

"Try"

This word does not break rapport as badly as "but" or the other words previously mentioned. I still avoid using it because this verb is a weak word and not effective in communication.

For example: "I will try to call you tonight." What does it mean to "try to call?" Either I will call or I won't call. To most people who hear it, it sounds like an excuse waiting to happen.

While writing this book, I kept searching for other words to use. Of course, in some cases, it might make sense to say, "Try the techniques in the book." Or "I want to try something new."

Even then, it sounds weak and gives the impression that the person does not have a very strong intention behind the words. Perhaps you would agree that it sounds better to say, "Practice the techniques in the book," or "I want to learn something new."

Words to Buy Time

In this fast-paced society, it is easy to feel pressured to keep up and to think fast. Especially when we are in a work situation, we want to appear effective and able to make quick decisions to impress others. In a business meeting, we may have agreed to carry out a task or meet a deadline that we realize later is impossible to do. In a personal situation, we may have agreed to do something before we have taken the time to think about it and make the best decision.

There are times when I know I am not feeling at my best and that I would rather not answer a question or make a commitment until I have sorted out my feelings about it. When I think about how I want to reply ahead of time, my response usually sounds better to the person hearing it than if I had replied on the spot.

For these reasons and more, certain phrases can help buy ourselves some time. Practice the phrases below to test whether you feel more or less powerful when you say them to other people.

"I'm not sure. Let me think about it and get back to you."

This is a perfectly acceptable response for anyone wanting an answer from you. Whether it is a job offer, or a marriage proposal, it is definitely reasonable to ask for time to think about something, and come back later with a decision. It is reasonable, honest, direct and does not hurt anyone's feelings. At the same time, we can buy time to figure out the best way to proceed and the best words to use at a later time.

I have been practicing a similar response, "That is a good question. I haven't thought about it. Let me get back to you on that." I use this in specific situations and with certain people so that I do not react with an impulsive response that I might regret later.

Even when we know immediately that we will turn the person down, statements like these buy us time so that we can think about what we really want to say. Extra time helps us to think about the best ways to communicate our decisions so that they do not hurt other people's feelings or cause political problems at work. Then, Pacing and Leading, presented earlier in this chapter, can help us to craft the most gracious responses.

"I Don't Know"

When another person wants a decision or your input about an issue or situation, it is fine to say, "I don't know." Initially, we might think that it will make us look weak and indecisive to say this, especially at work. Surprisingly, it often has the opposite effect and allows us to feel our power.

It is okay not to know the answer right then and there. Sometimes it takes time to figure out what we really think about something.

Then, it may take more time and more thought to put it into words. Usually after a short time, the answers appear in our minds, and we can find the best words to explain our position without offending another person.

"Why do you ask?"

I love to use this response when people ask me a question that I do not want to answer. Sometimes when we are asked personal questions, we might be taken by surprise. Since we are off-guard, we might say something that we did not mean or would have preferred to have kept to ourselves.

The response, "Why do you ask?" answers the question with another question, and does two things for us. First, it buys time so I can think about what I really want to say. Second, it suggests very tactfully that it is really none of the other person's business. This question conveys curiosity and does not hurt anyone's feelings. When I use this response, the conversation often moves in a completely different direction so there is no need to answer the original question.

Some people may ask the same question a second time. The

next statement can help when someone is persistently asking about something that you would rather not discuss.

"I would prefer not to discuss that right now."

Whenever someone asks a question that you would prefer not to answer, this is an appropriate response. The power in this simple statement is revealed when the other person tends to apologize after hearing this reasonable response.

I can think of times that I wish I would have used this response instead of answering a question and discussing people or situations that I would have preferred not to discuss. I can think of parties and gatherings that I would have enjoyed more if I had used these simple words.

This concludes the section on improving communication, which is one way to Choose Power with People. Listen to the specific words used in conversations to appreciate their effects. Practice some of these to discover how well they work for you.

The rest of the chapter discusses ways to set effective boundaries. This is a helpful way to experience power in situations in which another person is difficult or wants to manipulate us.

Effective Boundaries with People

Effective power with people includes knowing how to improve communication, how to set boundaries and how to end a relationship completely, if needed. Having the full set of tools and techniques to draw from allows us to choose the best one to use in a specific situation.

Many of us have not been taught how to limit or end a relationship with another person, so making the decision might feel uncomfortable. However, these are perfectly acceptable options. We all possess limited time, energy and resources in our life. There is no reason to continue putting energy into a relationship that makes us feel bad or powerless.

If we cannot end a relationship completely because the other person is a relative or co-worker who we will continue to see, we can still change the "rules" that operate in a relationship, and therefore set new boundaries.

After reading through these next sections, you will be aware of your options and can better decide how to proceed. Maybe you will decide to change the rules and boundaries, and then re-assess the relationship later. If the situation improves, that is fantastic.

If, on the other hand, when you re-assess the relationship, you decide that it is still adding more stress to your life than you want, then you might choose to end the relationship. If so, the Power of No Attention (Extinction) section, which follows this section, explains how to do that.

Changing the Rules

A relationship with a particular person may be difficult or cause you stress for a variety of reasons. If you can boil the issue down to a specific behavior that someone is doing (or not doing), then it makes it easier to discuss and to address.

For example, Shirley is upset that her son comes home later than he says he will. Marvin gets mad when his wife calls him when he is in important meetings.

In each of these examples, a specific behavior is identified. Now, how can we change the "rules" so that the behavior and its consequences are not a problem? Meet with all the people involved so that everyone is empowered to participate in choosing the new rule together. The best outcomes occur when everyone is happy with the "rule."

For example, Shirley and her son agree that he will be grounded for one full day every time he is more than 10 minutes late. She explains that being "grounded" means that he cannot leave the house and that she will take his cell phone away from him. Marvin and his wife agree that she will email him instead of calling. He promises to call her right back if he is not in a meeting.

In both situations, a new rule that targets the problem behavior is agreed upon by everyone involved. Implement the new rule consistently to check whether it solves the problem. For example, it will not work if Shirley does not follow through with the consequences the next time that her son is late, or if Marvin does not respond to his wife's emails as promised.

After a few weeks, review whether the change has been working. If it is working well, continue using the rule. If it is not working well, then it might be necessary to meet again with all of the people who are involved, and find another rule to implement.

I have a friend who is very good at setting boundaries like this. For example, one day, she and her brother decided they no longer wanted to hear the criticisms that their uncle said about them to their mother. Their mother had been repeating negative comments that her brother said about them for all of their lives. After years of having their feelings hurt, the brother and sister took action by asking their mother to stop repeating what their uncle said about them.

At that point, it is up to the mother. She could agree to be the filter between the conversations. In other words, she could agree to hear the comments from her brother, and not repeat them to her children. If she cannot agree to this, then another option is for her to ask her brother to stop saying negative things about her children. In this way, she is refusing to be the one to filter information. She is passing the boundary on to the brother.

Consistent Boundaries

Consistency is very important when implementing a boundary. Regardless of what the mother decides, it is up to the brother and sister to stop their mother the next time that she begins to cross the boundary. Reminders may be needed until everyone is used to the new rule.

Habits and behaviors take some time to change. The reminder does not have to be unkind, just firm. For example, a simple statement such as, "Mom, we agreed not to talk about that," and changing the subject, works well.

If the mother was the one who set the boundary with her brother, then she also has to be firm and consistent. The next time her brother starts to criticize her children, she can say something like, "Let's talk about something else."

Another way to set a natural boundary with another person is to say No to someone's request. The next section will assist those of us who have difficulty saying No.

The Power to Say No

If you are good at saying No to other people, then feel free to skip this section. This section is for those of us who have NOT been successful at turning down other people when we have secretly wanted to do so.

Many of us have been taught to be polite, or to sacrifice our needs for other people. Perhaps we find it hard to refuse another person without feeling guilty or afraid of losing the other person's love and approval.

It is important to realize that we each have the right to say No. We obviously cannot do everything for everyone. We have limits to our time, money, and other resurces.

Setting boundaries is natural and normal, and saying No is one way to do that. Greater self-respect and self-confidence are achieved when we deliver strong and consistent No's to other people when necessary because we are prioritizing our time in order to stick to our life plan and values.

When we stop and think about the costs and benefits before we make a decision, we might conclude that it is best for us to say No. As long as we say No with respect and courtesy, we have no reason to feel badly or guilty for it. No apologies are necessary.

These are the three steps to say No effectively.

1) Use Words to Buy Time (from earlier in this chapter) to think about the request.
2) List the advantages and disadvantages, using the following Pros and Cons technique.
3) Practice Pacing and Leading to find a gracious way to say No.

In Step 1, we ask for some time to think about the request so we can check in with ourselves before we say Yes. Many times, I have agreed to something before taking the time to think it through. "Let me think about it," and other statements from the Words to Buy Time section earlier in this chapter help. The purpose of buying time is to use it to make a good decision, and then to plan a gracious way to say No, if needed.

The second step is to use the Pros and Cons technique to list the advantages and benefits, and then the disadvantages and costs. Every time we agree to do one thing, it takes time and energy away from doing something else. This technique will help us to see it all outlined on paper.

Take two pieces of paper and draw lines down the center of the pages. On one piece of paper, list all of the benefits and advantages to saying Yes to the request on the left side of the line. On the right side of the line, list the disadvantages and the costs of saying Yes. On the second piece of paper, list the benefits to saying No on the left side of the line; on the right side of the line list the disadvantages and the costs of saying No. When we see it all outlined on paper, it is often clear what the best choice is.

Finally, if we decide that it is in our best interest to say No, the third step is to design a gracious way to turn down the request. Some people prefer saying a simple, "No, I don't think so," and leaving it at that without further explanation. Others choose to explain further, and the Pacing and Leading section earlier in this chapter can help us design a suitable response. Some examples follow.

Terry's friend asked him to help him move early one Saturday morning. He worked through the steps above and realized that he would resent his friend if he agreed to wake up early on the only day of the week that he can sleep late. He was motivated to find a good way to say No to that request. He said he could not help in the morning, and offered to help later in the day.

Betty was offered a promotion to a new job with a higher salary. She asked for time to think about it. After outlining the costs and benefits, she realized that if she accepted the promotion she would have to give up family time and her book group. By implementing this technique, she was able to find the right words to turn down the promotion because it was in her best interests.

This way of setting boundaries helps us, as well as helping others. Those who have raised or worked with children know how they will continue to push for more and more, until we say No. In fact, they make us set a limit for them because they need boundaries. Although it may be more subtle, adults do the same thing. Adults, like children, sometimes need to know how far they can push and may continue to test our boundaries for their own comfort level. Some people may take us for granted and even lose respect for us until we have set effective boundaries with them. For example, once we have agreed to organize a Bake Sale, others may expect us to do it every year.

There are other ways to set boundaries with people that are more subtle. The next couple of sections discuss how to Choose Power in certain situations simply by not participating in them.

The Power of Non-Participation

Non-participation occurs when we skip what everyone else is doing in order to follow our own intuition. It is taking a stand to make our own decisions and choose our own perceptions. There are many examples of non-participation.

For example, in an office setting, maybe everyone is gossiping, and Vanessa chooses to walk away and go back to work because she does not want to talk about co-workers behind their backs. In addition to making her feel powerful, other people pick up on the message and are positively affected at a subtle level. Whether or not other people respond, we feel powerful when we make our own choices.

I am reminded about a story I read about women who were meeting together. A group of men arrived outside of the house and seemed about to harass the women. The women agreed on a plan of non-participation.

When the men stormed into their meeting place in an effort to disrupt and intimidate the women, the women just sat in a circle looking at each other, holding hands. Instead of showing fear, the women ignored the men completely and acted as if they were not even there. They only looked at each other, and did not look at the men or acknowledge that they were there. The men ranted and raved for a brief time before leaving, because they got no reaction from the women. The women resumed what they were doing.

Isn't that an incredible story about taking power back instead of giving it up? One group simply refused to acknowledge that another group had any power over them. If the women had reacted in fear, they would have given the men the power they expected, and the story would have had a completely different outcome. Instead, the women chose not to participate in the intention of the men, which was to intimidate and disrupt their meeting.

I love the simplicity of this story. I can think of other examples of situations in which a variation of this story would be truly effective. Can you?

Mahatma Gandhi and Martin Luther King Jr both used forms of non-participation to bring about dramatic social changes. These great leaders encouraged people to join together to change the unfair cultural practices that fostered discrimination. It worked and they changed history. We will discuss these leaders again in greater depth in the Power of Love section in Chapter 7.

These examples offer practical ways to not participate in a situation that is happening around us. Another way to Choose

Power is to not respond to what is being said. The next section explains how the Power of Silence can be used during conversations.

The Power of Silence

One technique I like to use when I am talking with someone who I do not like or do not trust is to be quieter than I usually am in conversations. Sometimes, instead of responding, I can feel more power by not responding. This choice allows the other person to continue to talk and reveal thoughts, feelings and intentions throughout the conversation, while I simply listen in silence.

This increases my personal power because I have more information about that person. If I am asked about my silence, I use neutral phrases, such as "I am not feeling talkative today," or "I am just thinking about what you are saying," or "I will get back to you when I have had some time to think about this conversation."

"Silence is the ultimate weapon of power."
- Charles de Gaulle

Be warned, people are not used to us listening in silence. It might make others feel uncomfortable, even as it helps me to feel more powerful. The other person may do what he or she can to get me to talk. A non-committal response like, "I am not sure, let me think about it," or other suggested responses from the Words to Buy Time section earlier in this chapter can help.

This concludes the section on setting effective boundaries, which provided a range of techniques to use at work or at home. Setting boundaries is a great first step with a difficult person. However, if you come to the conclusion that you would prefer not to have this person in your life, then the next section provides the details needed to effectively end a relationship with someone.

Power of No Attention

When we have done everything we can to improve a relationship with someone and it has not worked, limiting or ending a relationship might be appropriate. Whether or not we see this person on a daily basis, we can minimize the attention and energy we give that person, using extinction.

We have heard about the dinosaurs going "extinct." This means that they no longer exist. In behavioral psychology, "extinction" means to make a behavior exist no longer. I can use extinction with children to end certain, specific behaviors. With stalkers, I can use extinction to end all contact.

First, I will present examples to illustrate the principles of extinction, because it requires a bit of understanding and commitment before using the technique. Next, we will address complete extinction, which is useful for someone like a stalker. After that, Modified Extinction is presented for situations in which you want to keep a person in your life. For example, it works well with children.

Example One - What We Do for Attention

The underlying assumption of extinction is that human beings are social creatures and thrive on attention from others. Many things that we do are done to get the attention of another person.

I used this principle when I used to write behavior management programs for mentally retarded adults in Louisiana group homes and had great success. From this point of view, we assume that almost every problem behavior exists because it gets attention from someone.

For example, if a client hits his head on a wall long enough or hard enough, a staff member will come over to get him to stop. This might be the only way the client can get the staff to come over and give some needed attention. We all thrive on attention from other people because we experience feelings of power.

Therefore, my Behavior Management Program was written to

encourage staff to interact with the man whenever he was NOT hitting his head on the wall. Whenever he WAS hitting his head on the wall, staff would put a helmet on the person and ignore him. The client learned that he got more attention when he did not bang his head on the wall, and so the problem behavior stopped.

This process works with all people. What do YOU do to get attention from others? Some of us like to call friends or family if we feel lonely. Many of us like to tell good stories or jokes to get attention from a group at the office or at a dinner party. I like to go up to my partner for a hug and a kiss. We all use different ways to get attention.

Getting someone's attention feels good and rewarding to us. It is like we are flowers in a garden and the other person is watering us with a garden hose. We thrive on and need attention from other people on a regular basis, just like flowers need water to thrive. We grow strong from the loving support we receive from other people, and may feel like we are "wilting" if we feel rejected by someone else.

Whose gardens are you watering with your garden hose of nourishing energy and power? Once you realize that you have limits to the energy that you give away to other people, you might decide to turn off the garden hose of attention for someone at any time. Withdrawing your attention from someone who is used to receiving your nourishing energy has serious effects. The nature of the relationship will shift significantly, as explained in more detail below.

Conclusion: We say and do many things to get attention from others. Attention from other people feels good.

Example Two - Using Extinction with Someone
Extinction works by turning off that garden hose of attention. Completely remove all of your attention. This includes stopping

telephone calls, emails, notes and all other forms of communication. I have used this technique with a variety of people ranging from bothersome people in the office, to a nasty man in my social circle, to a boyfriend who became a stalker after I broke up with him. Extinction worked well in every case. It will work for you, too, as long as you are prepared for the results, which are extremely predictable.

Many of us, especially women, have been brought up to be polite. If someone calls and asks us to call back, we might return the call, out of courtesy. However, if it is someone who you have decided to break-up with or stop seeing for any reason, you have every right to ignore the phone call completely. Because it is not something that we have been told we can do, or taught how to do, it may take a while to get used to ignoring the request to call back, and dealing with the feelings that accompany that decision.

What if you have decided to end a relationship and the other person will not leave you alone? The best thing to do is to stop interacting with him or her completely. Do not return the phone calls. Do not agree to meet for lunch "for one last time." If you truly want this person out of your life, remove your attention completely from him or her.

If you see the person at a social event, turn your back to him or her, and pretend that you do not know the person at all. If your social "rules" dictate that you acknowledge the person, briefly say "Hi," or nod in their direction, and then calmly move away from the person. No need to make any conversation. The point is to make the experience as non-pleasurable and non-rewarding for the other person as possible.

Here is an example. One man in my social circle got my email address and asked me out on a date. When I turned him down, he sent me a nasty email, insulting me and calling me names. I remember that I was shaking after I read it.

I decided to use extinction with him. Whenever I saw him at a party, I turned my back or walked right past him, without acknowledging that I knew him. If he joined the circle I was chatting with, I said "Excuse me," and left the group.

Perhaps you think this is severe. On the other hand, what did I owe this person, especially after that nasty email that he sent me? Why would I pretend that he was worthy of my limited time and energy? I had nothing positive to say to him, I would prefer him to stay away from me and my friends.

Using extinction produced the results I desired. He left me alone. In fact, I only needed to deliberately act like this (turn my back on him, walk away) a couple of times for him to get the message. The fantastic result is that he proceeded to avoid me at all of the next parties. I loved that. I didn't need to endure the nervous heart palpitations any more when I saw him. I could relax and enjoy the party, even if he was there. The situation naturally took care of itself. To this day, we just walk right past each other.

Conclusion: Removing attention from people is the key to using extinction.

Example Three - Negative Attention is Better than No Attention

Let's continue with the garden hose analogy where we water other people's flowers with our attention. If I decide to stop watering with my garden hose, and my neighbor who is washing his car pours the bucket of water into the garden, the flowers will use that water for nourishment. Although the flowers might prefer unpolluted water, they will use what they can from any water so that they may continue to thrive.

This is true for people, too. Although people prefer loving and positive attention from other people, if they cannot get attention that way, they might use other ways to water their flower gardens.

In other words, while positive attention waters people's gardens, negative attention, such as yelling and screaming, will also water gardens. Negative attention is a different type of watering hose that works just as well as positive attention for certain people. Perhaps you know children who get in trouble over and over again. They have learned that negative attention is better than no attention at all.

Here is another example. One man who I broke up with began stalking me, so I used extinction with him. I removed my attention from him completely and did not return his calls or emails.

Because I stopped watering his garden with my hose of positive attention, he needed to find some other way to water his flowers. Somehow this man found out both of my parents' unlisted phone numbers and started to call them on the phone and tell them lies about me.

Initially, I could not understand why he did that. Of course, I would not have dated him again after that, so that could not have been his motive.

I finally realized that if he was not going to get loving, positive attention from me anymore, he hoped that I would still call him and yell at him for telling lies to my parents. He needed someone to water his flowers. Even though people prefer good attention over bad attention, bad attention is better than no attention at all.

That is why it is important to turn off the garden hose completely. Strong negative emotions, like anger, will still water his or her garden. Showing NO emotion is the most effective way to apply extinction.

In the next two examples, we will understand how yelling and screaming would have made the situation worse for me than ignoring the stalker completely.

Conclusion: Turn off good attention and bad attention completely when using extinction with someone.

Example Four - The Extinction Burst

One very important fact to realize is that once you begin to use extinction with someone, for a short time the other person may contact you more. This is called an Extinction Burst. It is predictable and happens almost every time, so be prepared for an immediate increase in the number and types of contacts that the other person will attempt to have with you. As long as you expect it, it's not so surprising or shocking when it happens.

If we think about it for a minute, we can understand why this happens. For example, Jack is used to calling Jill and feeling like his flowers are being watered when she calls back. When she does not call back, his flowers begin to wither. So, he calls again and she does not call back. Now the flowers are dying and he feels more desperate to get the nourishment that he is used to getting.

This is a crucial time and is called the Extinction Burst. Jack will do everything he can think of, whether it is calling, stopping by her house or catching her as she is leaving the office. Only when he is convinced that no more water is coming from Jill will he finally stop bothering her, and perhaps turn to someone else to get his flowers watered. When that happens, the Extinction Burst has passed.

The Extinction Burst is a very important time in the extinction process. If Jill successfully avoids contact with the person during the Extinction Burst, then his contacts stop. Jack may never bother her again.

On the other hand, if Jack succeeds in getting to see Jill during the Extinction Burst, and receives some positive or negative attention from her, then things could get worse, because his attempts have been reinforced or rewarded. He has learned that as long as he keeps making attempts, he will eventually be successful at getting some kind of attention. As we now know, negative attention is better than no attention at all.

Remember my stalker story? When the man realized that he was getting no response, he continued to call my answering machine and left messages and kept talking until he used up the entire tape!

The best response to this Extinction Burst is to ignore it, so the behavior ends. I experienced success using this approach, and it will work the same for anyone who succeeds in withholding positive and negative attention during this crucial time.

Conclusion: Be prepared for the Extinction Burst and know that this is the most important time to stop all attention toward that person.

Example Five - The Child Screaming for Candy in the Check-out line

Here is another example that might help. We have all seen and heard the child at the check-out wanting some candy. The best response is for the parent to firmly say "No," and change the subject so the child starts thinking about something else. It is best to completely ignore any screaming tantrums that follow, if possible. If the parent does this consistently every time, the child will eventually stop crying for candy at the check-out.

On the other hand, if the child screams louder, and the parent gives in and buys some candy, then the child has learned that screaming loud is the key to getting candy. What will the child do the next time they are at the checkout? Get the earplugs, because the screaming could be very loud.

The same thing applies to a stalker. If he calls a woman four times and she lets the machine take the call, and then she answers on the fifth phone call and says, "Stop calling me! Leave me alone!" it is probably the worst thing to do. (Well, going to bed with the person again is probably the worse thing she can do!) She has just taught the stalker that he needs to call at least five times in a row in order to get her attention, and then she will water his flowers. As a result, he has learned to call five times in a row, perhaps several times every day to get some water for his flowers. You see, she now has a worse problem on her hands.

Conclusion: The amount and intensity of the contacts will increase if the person receives attention during the Extinction Burst.

Summary

To review, we learned the following:

1) We say and do many things to get attention from others. Attention from other people feels good.
2) Removing attention from people is the key to using extinction.
3) Turn off good attention and bad attention completely when using extinction with someone.
4) Be prepared for the Extinction Burst and know that this is the most important time to stop all attention for that person.
5) The amount and intensity of the contacts will increase if the person receives attention during the Extinction Burst.

Understanding these principles is more important than anything else in this book. Before we decide to use extinction, we need to be committed to following through with it once we start. Especially with a stalker, it is easy to create a worse situation.

Here is another example. If a woman ignores a stalker for a month, and then she wants to see him and agrees to have lunch with him, then she has just taught the stalker to persist for at least a month next time, because she will eventually agree to see him. As you can see, this can easily make the problem worse the next time that she thinks she is serious about avoiding contact. She will endure at least a full month of being bothered. Therefore, only use extinction when you have decided you want no more contact and are ready to follow through and consistently apply the technique.

If you have significant concerns about personal safely, please get yourself some help. This is important. Tell all of your friends and family about your problem so that they can help and support you. Contact the police and the nearest Domestic Violence shelter. Ask about a restraining order.

I also recommend the excellent book, *The Gift of Fear* by Gavin de Becker. He tells many stories and explains how to predict how violent a person will be. It is difficult to put down because it is so captivating. It has saved many lives, including mine, which I will go into in greater depth in the Power and Safety section at the end of this chapter.

If you are using extinction for the first time, a trained therapist can help. You may have mixed feelings about ending a relationship with someone. That is normal. People typically go through a grieving period whenever a relationship comes to an end. That is also normal. The Releasing Heavy Heart Energy, which is the first technique in Chapter 4, is extremely helpful for a situation like this.

If you decide that you want to use extinction with a stalker, the next checklist will help you to prepare before you begin to apply the technique. Take the opportunity to complete it to make sure that you are ready for what you will face BEFORE you start using extinction with someone like a stalker.

Technique 2 – Pre-Extinction Checklist

This checklist is helpful to go through before using extinction. It is especially important to use it for a stalker or another person who could possibly by violent or dangerous. Be sure to tailor the questions to best apply to your specific situation.

For simplicity, I have used male pronouns in the next technique since most stalkers are men. However, female stalkers do exist, so use this information and checklist for anyone, regardless of their gender.

---

1) What can this person do to get you to take them back? Think long and hard about this one. If you come up with ANYTHING here, then please do not begin to use extinction with this person because it will not work. There will be a part of you that secretly still wants to take back the other person, and that part of you will sabotage your efforts to avoid this person.

☐ No matter what this person does, I will not let this person back into my life.

2) On paper, list all of the ways that this person has contacted you in the past. Next, prepare a response for each one so that you are prepared the next time that the person contacts you in this way. For example, if he calls you, you will check the caller ID and not take the call if it is him. As you prepare a response for every situation, remember that the best responses are those that minimize attention and end contact as soon as possible.

☐ I am prepared with a response if this person contacts me in the same ways as in the past.

3) List every other way you can think of that he could attempt to contact you or get your attention. Imagine anything that a desperate person might think of, because he is likely to become desperate during the Extinction Burst. Put every possible situation on a separate line. Could you see him at certain Happy Hours, grocery stores, coffee shops, parties or other places? Does this person have contact with your friends? Brainstorm with other people until you have

thought of every possibility of what might happen and what he might do to come in contact with you.

4) For each method of contact on your list from Step 3, prepare a response as you did in Step 2. In case it actually happens, you will be prepared to minimize and end contact. For example, if he shows up at a place where you like to go every week, simply say "Please don't come here to see me," and walk away. Remember, it is most important to say this in a neutral tone of voice. If the stalker sees that he upset you, it will "water his flowers." Walk away and avoid the person if he does not leave the place.

☐ I am prepared with a response if this person contacts me in other ways than in the past.

5) In your head, imagine each situation you listed on paper for Steps 2 through 4. Visualize yourself in each situation acting confidently and successfully all the way through to the end. Once you have prepared for each situation and practiced ahead of time in your head, you will be ready and not as surprised if it happens in real life. Research shows that the brain and the body react the same way whether a situation is happening in real life or whether it is imagined. Therefore, you have trained your body and mind how to react if that situation ever really occurs.

☐ I have visualized my success and am ready to begin extinction.

Extinction Example at Work

As we have already discussed in the past section, complete extinction is necessary to successfully remove a stalker from one's life. The garden hose needs to be completely turned off. However, there are times that a relationship cannot be ended so abruptly. At work, we may continue to see another person, although we might prefer not to have contact. It is important to realize that we still have the power to control the nature of daily interactions with anyone.

Take a moment and really think about whether you want to use extinction with this person before you decide to start this, because it really works. The results will be fewer conversations and fewer interactions with that person. Are there times when you will miss chatting with this person? Sometimes it is still more fun to talk with an annoying person to break-up the work situation. If that is the case for you, then do not use extinction.

If you have decided that you truly want to reduce the amount of interactions with someone at work, here are the essential steps. Turn off that garden hose of attention toward him or her. Avoid the person as much as you can. Do not respond every time the person says something to you. Do not initiate conversations. Talk about work only, and do not discuss personal topics.

Every situation is different, and sometimes this becomes a whole lot easier than you might think. I know, because I have had the opportunity to use this technique successfully in work situations.

I remember one co-worker in particular who was very self-absorbed. I was tired of him coming and sitting in my office and relating his personal woes to me when I was busy working. He was also very sarcastic. After enduring enough biting comments and negative interactions, I had had enough. I decided to use extinction with him.

I avoided him. I didn't say "Good morning," or "Goodbye," unless he did. I walked away or ended our conversations as nicely as I could, as quickly as I could.

I became more aware of my power. I learned that I had the freedom all along to just stand up and leave my office even if he was sitting there, or to turn back to my computer, or to walk away from a conversation with a simple, "excuse me," whenever I chose.

The point is to make all interactions non-rewarding for the other person and to avoid the person whenever possible. Showing the person no emotion is the most efficient and effective way to apply extinction. Turn off the garden hose and all visible emotions completely. If I had shown an emotion like anger, disgust or frustration to him, it would have backfired.

Some of you may think that my behavior does not sound very nice. I do admit that it feels different to avoid a person. However, I was much happier at work whenever he left me alone, so I knew that it was important to my well-being that I use extinction with him.

As a result of my reduced interactions with this co-worker, I experienced tremendous success and felt incredible personal power. He no longer came into my office to discuss his latest relationship and landlord stories, and I was much happier for that. He went off in pursuit of another audience, and luckily he found it. They all watered each other's gardens. My whole opinion of my job changed. Everybody was much happier.

That is one of the beauties of extinction: it works every time!

Modified Extinction

We learned that for a stalker or other potentially dangerous people, it is best to turn off the hose and ignore the person completely. Those of you who have understood everything so far may be ready for this next technique that becomes a bit more complicated. Although it is much easier to completely turn off the garden hose than to do Modified Extinction, this technique works well for people you want to keep in your life. For example, this technique reduces problem behavior in children.

The next section shows how to ignore undesired behavior, and to give positive attention to the person when he or she is well-behaved. If you need to read this section several times to fully understand it, it will be well worth the effort because you will learn how you affect another person's behavior. In other words, we can turn our hose of attention on when they are acting "right," and turn it off for certain target behaviors. Although this technique works well with children, the next story shows how well it works with adults.

Example – Someone saying suggestive statements to me

I began this chapter with the story of a man in my social circle. He is very popular and attends just about every party I do, because he is in every social circle that I am. I do not dislike him as a person; however, I did dislike the crude, sexual remarks that he used to say to me regularly.

Here is how I successfully stopped his suggestive and inappropriate statements. Whenever I saw him, I would give him a hug, and greet him. I would continue talking to him until he said something that I considered to be inappropriate or offensive. At that point, I immediately turned away from him and started talking to someone else, or walked away after saying, "That's disgusting." I consistently did this every single time that it happened.

The Extinction Burst occurred, of course. Once or twice, he said crude remarks immediately upon seeing me. If he did, I still continued using the technique on him every time it happened.

It is important to understand that if I had not followed through with the technique one or twice, this inconsistency would have caused him to increase the undesired behavior. This is known as "intermittent reinforcement" which makes the situation worse. (Although a complete explanation of intermittent reinforcement is beyond the scope of this book, I recommend learning more about it because it explains why addictive behaviors, such as gambling, are so difficult to stop.)

In a short time, this man learned not to make the crude remarks until later in the conversation. I still walked away. Eventually he stopped altogether. Although I imagine that he still makes inappropriate comments to other women in my social circle, he no longer says them to me. Now, I can chat with him at parties without having to endure comments I find disgusting. However, I am prepared that if he does say something inappropriate to me again, I need to walk away. There is a possibility that this can happen, since I chose to keep him in my life.

Therefore, the ingredients for success are to pick the target behavior and to consistently follow the technique. Give the person attention until the behavior occurs. As soon as the target behavior occurs, immediately turn away and stop giving attention for a couple of minutes. With children, pull your hose of attention away and turn it towards someone or something else for at least 60 seconds. If the problem behavior disappears, then you may turn your attention back to the child. Continue until the problem behavior happens again. Be consistent and you will notice that the problem behavior goes away. Although you are aware of what you are doing, the other person will never realize it.

One Kindergarten teacher turned her entire classroom around by using this technique. She ignored the "bad" behaviors and gave a lot of attention to the "good" behaviors that she wanted in her classroom by praising the good behavior in front of everyone whenever it occurred. Eventually, all the children wanted to do the good behaviors to get the attention and get their flowers watered by her hose.

Remember what you learned about the Extinction Burst: if you are not prepared to carry out your program consistently, the situation may become worse. If you let the person "get away with it" just one time, the behavior problem may increase, until you are ready to apply this technique consistently.

Extinction is an extremely powerful technique. Use it with caution because:

1) It works, and
2) It may make a problem behavior much worse until you are committed to following through with it each and every time.

Power and Safety

Just as dealing with a stalker may threaten our safety, we do not know when we might find ourselves in an unexpected situation with dangerous people. Therefore, it is good to be prepared for any threatening situations that could happen in the future.

In an unfamiliar environment, or somewhat threatening situation, our adrenaline kicks in with the resulting "fight or flight" response. The body gets geared up to fight or to run and the mind does not seem to work so well.

Therefore, one thing to remember is our power to not participate in that situation. Remind yourself NOW to remember THEN that the words "NO" and "STOP" are the best first responses that attackers do not expect. Hearing yourself shouting words like this also gives you confidence in the moment when you need it.

A second suggestion is to give yourself an incredible gift and read *The Gift of Fear* by Gavin de Becker as soon as you can. Not only is it so well-written that it is hard to put down, it is also incredibly empowering. After finishing it, people have more confidence in themselves and their bodies. We are convinced that in a truly fearful situation, our bodies will react to save us. Knowing that allows us to drop fear that has no cause, and only feel it when we are truly in danger.

My Example in Los Angeles

Luckily, I had read the book long before I took a trip to LA with a friend. Four of us had attended dinner and a play together and stayed late afterwards chatting with the actors.

Stan was driving and he pulled over to get gas on the way home. Stan stuck his head in the car to tell us that he felt nervous because someone had just approached him asking for money, and he felt threatened after he turned him down. His wife did not seem to understand that we were in danger and asked him to wash the windows anyway.

Meanwhile, I had been watching the people in the car parked behind us because they were acting in a peculiar way. First of all, the people were completely focused on us and watching us. Secondly, one man was working frantically with something on the floor under his steering wheel. Finally, I saw him rush out of the car towards Stan.

I didn't even think. I trusted my body to act. I flew out of our car and ran around towards the two men and clapped my hands loudly and said "NO!"

The man from the other vehicle stopped and looked confused. Then, another passenger in our car got out of our car and started following the stranger to the car behind us, toward whatever trap had been set up under the steering wheel.

I begged my friend to please get back in our car. I thank my lucky stars that he listened to me and we all got safely back out on the road.

On the way to the highway, we drove past a large group of men who had been hiding in the shadows. Seeing weapons, we realized that they had been watching us and planning for us to be their next victims.

The bottom line is that I truly believe that the information I learned in *The Gift of Fear* saved all of our lives that night. The book persuaded me that my body would know exactly what to do in a threatening situation. It did.

I am now convinced that I can trust myself to act in a similar situation so that I do not carry useless fear around with me, worrying about what I would do in a situation like that. Looking back, I never would have thought that I had the power to act as I did. Luckily, I did not need to stop and think at all. Instead, I can trust my body to act in my best interest if I am ever again in a dangerous situation. Read that book so you have the same confidence in yourself.

The Power of Self-Defense

Self-defense is a tremendous addition to your collection of tools and techniques for having Power with People. Whether or not you are concerned on a daily basis about being a victim of crime, learning to defend ourselves is an important skill. We might need to defend ourselves or a loved one at any time.

There are several kinds of martial arts classes to choose from, such as karate, judo, kick-boxing, tae kwon do and so on. There may be one type that suits you the best.

Getting a good recommendation is a great place to start. I recommend seeing a class in action before you sign up. As in all teacher-student relationships, it is important to feel comfortable with the instructor and his or her approach. It can be more fun to join with a friend because you can support each other when it seems easier to go home and lie on the couch.

This type of class is so powerful because it might be the first time that you have ever been taught the correct way to hit or kick someone. Most women (and some men) have never had the opportunity to practice defending ourselves. We need to learn and practice how to punch and kick in self-defense, in case it is ever needed. In addition, it makes us feel more powerful in our bodies because it is good exercise.

A former boyfriend sponsored me to take a Self-Defense class while I was in my 20's because he knew it was a good investment.

Men might consider sponsoring the women you love in the same way.

At the end of the class, I had the opportunity to break a piece of wood with my bare hand. There is nothing in the world as empowering as that!

I have heard about a new seminar in which the participants break a board during the weekend. My friend who returned from this seminar reported that she had never felt as powerful as she did when she broke the board with her bare hands.

The bottom line is to do whatever makes you feel more confident and more powerful with people. Once the body has been taught to defend itself, it can access this knowledge at any time in our lives to protect us.

Summary

We have covered a lot in this chapter to help us to realize and remember our Power with People. Choose Power by improving conversational techniques, using or avoiding certain words, setting effective boundaries and using extinction when needed.

The Power and Safety section suggested that the body knows what to do, even when the mind does not. The next chapter discusses another way to access the Power of the Body.

CHAPTER 3

Power of the Body

"Every time you don't follow your inner guidance,
you feel a loss of energy,
loss of power,
a sense of spiritual deadness."
- Shakti Gawain

We feel powerful when our bodies feel good. Remember those mornings when you woke up feeling very good for no reason? There are mornings when I feel so powerful and vibrant in my body that I feel I am glowing.

Other times, if we are experiencing a significant health concern, it is easy to feel powerless. Sometimes we just need a simple answer about what our bodies need to feel better. When our bodies feel strong and healthy, we can feel powerful again.

For example, I came back from a beautiful and relaxing trip to Cozumel and I was feeling great. A couple days later, however, I came down with itchy insect bites. The itching was terrible and I could not sleep because they became very active at night. They kept moving around to different locations on my body, which was really creepy. I didn't know what kind of bugs they were. Finally, I went to the insect repellant section in my favorite health food store with my pendulum to find a remedy.

I asked my pendulum if there was something in front of me that would help. My pendulum responded Yes. I asked if it was on the first shelf and touched the shelf with my left hand. The pendulum responded No. I repeated with the second shelf. It said Yes. Then, I touched each remedy on the shelf, and proceeded to ask if each one was best for me, until it said Yes, and then I bought that product. Sure enough, it solved my problem and stopped the terrible itching.

This chapter begins with a discussion about the wisdom of the body. Next, we will understand how a pendulum can be used to communicate with our bodies to access the information that the body knows.

Wisdom of the Body

The body has tremendous wisdom and an incredible amount of resources to heal itself. The body knows exactly how to digest those truffles you've eaten, and what to do to repair a cut or a bruise on its body and so on.

The body's intelligence is also demonstrated when we are sick. For example, we are generally not hungry when we are sick. This is because the body is directing its energy towards healing itself instead of digesting food. It knows to decrease the hunger craving and to make us feel tired so that we will sleep a lot and heal ourselves. Animals in the wild experience this, too; they will go hide in a cave and sleep until they either get better or die.

The body knows how to do other amazing things. Those of you who have ever watched an animal give birth may have been amazed that she seems to know exactly what to do, although she has not done it before or taken any classes about it. For both animals and humans, often the body seems to take over and know exactly what to do.

The body has its own intelligence that appears unrelated to the intelligence of the mind. Have you heard about people who get premonitions about traveling and avoid accidents on trains and other vehicles? For example, the Titanic carried only 58 per cent of its passenger load. Several people, such as JP Morgan, cancelled their trips after dreaming that the ship was doomed.

Although some of the survivors also reported experiencing uneasy feelings before the trip, they chose to ignore these warnings and traveled anyway. This knowledge seems to be coming from the body, not the brain, because people talk about how they were FEELING. This suggests that the body somehow has access to its own knowledge.

Clearly, in all of these examples, the body has an intelligence of its own and seems to know what it needs to be healthy. The wisdom of the body may be a different type of knowledge than the wisdom in our minds. If so, both types of knowledge are important for our well-being.

I have found that the more I listen to what my body is telling me, the more it tells me. For example, my body lets me know when I am starting to come down with a cold or the flu. That helps because then I can take steps to stop the cold in its tracks if I act fast. I can feel where the cold is beginning to lodge itself in my body. If I feel it starting in my nose, I use an eye dropper to squirt salt water up my nose. If I feel it starting in my throat, I suck on a zinc lozenge and that knocks it right out of the body, so that I can avoid coming down with a cold or flu.

Every Body is Different

We may have heard over and over that everyone is different. I have heard health practitioners say, "There is no one right answer for everybody." Everyone has different needs, due to genetics, previous health challenges and so many other factors. Different people need different medications, food, vitamins, and so on. For example, we have different blood types and body types. Women have different hormones in their bodies than men have. Although one pill might help one person, it might cause a bad reaction in another person's body. Some people might need more Vitamin C than others because they are smokers.

Also, the body's needs may change from day to day. Some days my body might need a calcium supplement, while other days I may not need it because I ate a lot of spinach.

If only we could have access to the body's knowledge and find out answers about what is best for the body. What if the body could tell us which vitamins, herbs, foods, and other things are good for it right now, and which are not?

Communicating with the Body

The good news is that we do have ways to communicate with our bodies. Muscle testing is one method that some chiropractors and other health practitioners use to discover specific answers to questions about the needs of a person's body. The health practitioner can learn what techniques, or foods, or herbs or exercises that a person needs by asking the body questions. The body responds one way if the answer is Yes and another way if the answer is No.

The alternative health practitioners who use muscle testing swear that it works every time. The drawback is that two people are needed to do it.

What if I have a question I want to ask my body and no health practitioner is around? It seems like I ought to be able to obtain my own answers from my own body. I need a way for my body to communicate with me.

Pendulums to Increase Personal Power

A pendulum is a device that can communicate Yes and No responses about the body's current needs and other information, when used properly. As shown in the picture, one end hangs

down to swing freely. The other end is held between the thumb and closest two fingers of the dominant hand in order to include a positive, negative, and neutral energy.

When I ask a question, the pendulum responds to the energy of my body and swings one way to indicate Yes, or another way to indicate No. It is especially effective regarding questions about my body. I can quickly and easily determine what my body wants and needs at a particular moment in time.

The pendulum responds to knowledge that is available to all of us. People who are naturally intuitive get the same information without using a device like this. The pendulum just helps those of us who are not as intuitive.

At this point, let me offer the medical disclaimer that a pendulum is not approved by the AMA, and does not replace a qualified health practitioner, such as a naturopathic physician.

Later I will provide steps and techniques for using a pendulum so that you can learn to communicate with your body. Before we begin, here are some examples of ways to use a pendulum in everyday life:

~ Today, with all my vitamins, minerals and herbs in front of me, which ones do I need? Holding the pendulum in the right hand, touch each one with the left hand to find the ones needed today.

~ From a list of vitamins, minerals, herbs, etc, in a book, ask the pendulum, "Is there anything on this list that my body needs?" If the answer is Yes, ask if it is in this column or on this page. If the answer is Yes, then ask about each item until it says Yes.

~ What are the best foods for me to eat right now? Use a pendulum for foods on a menu and ask if salmon is best, or if a salad is best, etc.

~ Is my body intolerant of any foods that I eat?
Ask the pendulum about each food from a list to determine foods that are best to remove from the diet on a permanent or temporary basis.

~ In a health food store, ask, "Is there anything on this shelf that I need?" If the answer is No, go on to the next shelf and ask the same question. If the answer is Yes, touch each brand until the pendulum says Yes, as I did in the story at the beginning of the chapter.

~ As each body is unique and different from others, each brand of the same vitamin or herb is different from the rest. They may be made differently, stored differently, have different ingredients and so on. For example, I have figured out that potassium helps me to prevent migraines. Which one is the best for me? I can touch each brand of potassium with my left hand until the pendulum tells me the best brand for me. I have found that my pendulum usually prefers one product over the others as being best for me. And, it is not usually the most expensive product either.

~ Is this man / job / car / whatever else... best for me?
In addition to nutritional and supplemental concerns, a pendulum can be used to give a Yes or No answer about which jobs are best to apply for, which items are best to buy, and which people to date. It has a definite opinion. I have used a pendulum successfully while job-hunting and while choosing men from internet websites to meet in person.

~ Is my lost item in this closet? Is it in my car, etc.
My sister and I have had success in locating lost objects using a pendulum.

Good Questions to Ask
My favorite way to ask a question is to begin with "Is it best for me right now to..." If that does not work for your question, then keep the following in mind when forming your question.

First, the pendulum is best at answering Yes/No questions. It has limited power to communicate other information.

Second, the pendulum works best for questions about what is going on right now. What foods are good for my body right now? What vitamins or herbs are important right now?

It is not good at predicting the future. I believe this is because the future is uncertain and depends on many things. For example, what I eat for lunch might change what supplements I might need later tonight. My pendulum does not seem to know what herbs and supplements I need to take with me for an upcoming vacation.

Third, it is best to ask questions that are as clear as possible. If I am looking for a job and ask, "Is this a good job?" I may get a different answer than if I ask "Is it best for me to apply for this job?" or "Would I be happy working here?" Although it may sound incredible that the pendulum knows the answer to these questions, the body knows what is best for it, and my pendulum did help me pick out my last job in this way.

Finally, make sure that your questions are framed in the positive and do not have words like "Not" or "No" in them. The problem is that double negatives confuse everyone when we talk. Some examples are, "I can't not write" or "I won't say that I'm not disappointed." It takes some time to figure out what these sentences mean, and even then, they are unclear. In the same way, using negatives with a pendulum is confusing because, what does it mean if it says No to a question with a "not" in it? It becomes a double negative.

It is best to be as clear as possible. Therefore, remove the No's and the Not's from your questions. It is usually easy to drop the negative word in the question, and then change the sentence to its opposite. For example, "Is it not good for me to eat this pastry?" is better phrased as "Is it best for me to eat this pastry?" or "Is it best for me to avoid this pastry?"

Getting Started with a Pendulum

Pendulums are for sale in various stores and online (for example, type "pendulums for sale" at www.google.com). The tool can also

be made using a ring or a key hanging from some string, or a pendant on a necklace chain as shown in the picture. I have made my own at work using a paperclip and rubber band.

Hold one end of your pendulum with your right hand (or your dominant hand) and let the other end hang down so that it can swing freely. Use your thumb, first finger and second finger to hold the end. It is important that all three fingers are in contact with the end of the pendulum to provide a positive, negative, and neutral charge.

The pendulum needs to be able to swing freely in order to be able to communicate Yes and No answers by the way that it moves. It might swing clockwise for Yes and counterclockwise for No. Or, it might swing in a circle for Yes and move straight back and forth for No. Only you can determine how your pendulum communicates with you since it varies from person to person.

Practice the techniques below to have a great tool to communicate with your body. The more you practice, the more you will learn about yourself and about your pendulum.

Technique 1 – Pendulum and a Battery

Purpose: To experience your pendulum responding to external energy to see that it works.

This technique will give you confidence in the power of the pendulum to respond to energy.

---

1) Get into a relaxed state using the Calming Technique described in the first chapter.
2) Hang the pendulum over one end of a live battery. Notice that it begins to move in a circle.
3) Turn the battery over so the pendulum is hanging over the other end of the battery. Notice if it changes the way that it is moving and revolves in the other direction.

That was an easy and fun technique, wasn't it? The next technique will help you to learn how your pendulum will communicate with you. It does not swing the same way for everyone. Movements that indicate Yes and No responses vary from person to person.

Technique 2 – Pendulum Responses

Purpose: To discover what response from the pendulum means No and what response means Yes.

Now that you have the confidence that your pendulum responds to energy, it is time to find out how the pendulum will respond to your energy by asking it to communicate Yes and No to you.

1) Get into a relaxed state using the Calming Technique described in the first chapter.
2) Concentrate on Yes. Ask it to show you its Yes response. Ask it questions with answers that are definitely Yes, such as "Is my name ____?"
3) Concentrate on No. Ask it to show you its No response.

> Ask questions with answers that are definitely No, like "Do I live in Canada?" if you do not, or "Am I male?" if you are not.

If you have been able to make your pendulum work for you, congratulations! If not, it may take some time and persistence to get it to work for you. Some of the following suggestions may help.

Experiment with a different pendulum. It could be that the length is not the best for you, and you may need a longer or shorter one. Or perhaps the stone at the end of your pendulum does not work well with your energy. Choose another. Keep working at it. Ask a friend who uses a pendulum to pick out one that will work for you. Pendulums know whether they will work for a certain person or not, and they share that information when they are asked. That is how I found good pendulums for my mother and others who began to practice with the tools.

If you would prefer not to rely on a tool, here is an alternative. Deepak Chopra describes a similar technique in his book, *The Seven Spiritual Laws of Success*. He says to pay attention to your body when asking a Yes/No question. Either in your solar plexus or your heart, he says, you will feel a response. If it is a sensation of comfort, then the answer is Yes; if you feel discomfort, then the answer is No.

However, if you want to continue to practice with a pendulum, the following section contains additional tips. I worked for years with a pendulum before I was successful. (I tell the entire story in Chapter 5, Deciding Hard Enough.)

My mother, on the other hand, followed the steps in this chapter, and her pendulum responded immediately. She swears to me that it is right every time. Although she had been a skeptic about pendulums for years, once she made up her mind to use one, it responded immediately.

Additional Tips

~ You may sit or stand while using your pendulum. Do not cross your arms, legs, or ankles, because that blocks the energy flow through your body. Confusing or incorrect answers could result.

~ It is a good practice to "check in" with the pendulum and ask if the energy is flowing well before you ask a question. As noted previously, you might have your arms or legs crossed, or you might be near an energy source that would interfere with the proper energy flow needed by the pendulum. Also, sometimes facing a certain direction is preferred by the pendulum to communicate efficiently with you. For example, when I was in my apartment, it preferred for me to face west. If you ever have questions about these kinds of things, it is a good idea to ask your pendulum for guidance.

~ Phrase your questions precisely to be as clear as possible. For example, asking if someone is a "true friend" may not give you the information that you really want to know. Asking if you can trust this person or if the person has your best interests at heart are questions that are more specific. Be as clear as possible to get the real information that you desire.

~ Some people have had success asking for a third neutral communication that means, "I don't know," or "Ask again later." Feel free to go through Technique 2 an extra time to learn your third communication that represents a neutral answer. Concentrate on asking for a third movement that is completely different from the other two movements so that all three answers are clear to you.

~ Before I buy necklaces with a pendant, I like to ask whether or not they would make a good pendulum for me. They are honest and tell me the truth. I have had many tell me No.

~ If you get contradictory answers or other confusing responses from your pendulum, ask whether it has access to the information, and whether it is best for you to know the answers right now. Pendulums will let you know if this is true or not. Honor that.

Influencing Pendulum Responses

Some people are able to control how the pendulum swings with their minds. Everyone is different and it is not necessary to learn how to make your pendulum swing with your mind. Some people can influence it, some people cannot. What is important is finding our whether you can or not. Technique 3 (below) will let you test whether you can influence the swing of your own pendulum. This is important to know so that you can learn not to do that when you want a true answer.

For example, if I ask, "Is it best for me to eat chocolate right now?" I might have difficulty keeping my mind in a neutral place if I love chocolate. Some people can control the swing of the pendulum to get the answer they want and not the true answer.

If you are someone who can easily influence the pendulum's swing, it is important to know and to feel the difference when you are influencing it and when you are not. Therefore, if Technique 3 comes easily to you, it will be important for you to work through Technique 4.

Technique 3 – Influencing your Pendulum, or Not

Purpose: To learn whether you can control the swing of
your pendulum with your mind.

1) Get into a relaxed state using the Calming Technique
described in the first chapter.
2) Watch your pendulum and concentrate on Yes (or on
how it swings when it is telling you Yes) until you see it
respond with that swinging. Stop the swinging with
your hand and see if you can do it again.
3) Do the same thing with No. Concentrate on No (or on
how it swings when it is telling you No) until you see it
swing that way. Stop the swinging with your hand and
see if you can do it again.

How easy was it for you to make the pendulum move? Whether
or not you could influence the pendulum during Technique 3,
now you know this important information about yourself.
Express Self Gratitude for taking the time to learn this information.

If you were unable to affect the swing of your pendulum,
perhaps you cannot. My mother says that she cannot influence its
swing. Therefore, she reports that all of the answers that she
receives from her pendulum are from God and are not being
affected by her personal beliefs or desires.

If you fall into this group of people, then you can skip
Technique 4. It is actually easier for your group, because you
know that your pendulum answers are accurate, and not the
result of your desires or expectations.

If it was easy to influence the swing, then it is important to do
Technique 4, to notice the difference between the desire of your

mind and the energy of the body. Specifically, we need to feel the difference between influencing the pendulum to swing and allowing the pendulum to answer. It is a subtle difference that we can learn to feel.

Technique 4 – Accurate Pendulum Responses

Purpose: To learn when you are influencing the pendulum and when you are not.

If you learned from Technique 3 that you can influence your pendulum's movements, then it is important to understand what it feels like when you are influencing your pendulum and what it feels like when you are in a neutral, receiving mode. In other words, feel the difference between the two so that you can ensure that you are truly in a receiving mode when you are asking questions and not causing the pendulum to swing based on your expectations, beliefs or desires.

Your emotions are powerful and send out energy. They have the capacity to influence the swing of the pendulum. This technique will teach you how to feel the difference when you are influencing the pendulum and when you are open to its message. Although it may be a subtle difference, with practice you can easily feel it.

1) Get into a relaxed state using the Calming Technique described in the first chapter.
2) Ask your pendulum a factual question whose answer is Yes. Use your mind to force it to give you a No answer. That is, see if you can make your pendulum "lie" to you, or give you a wrong answer.

---

3) Now, ask your pendulum the same question and keep your mind in a neutral place and let it answer the question correctly with its swing.

4) The important goal here is to feel what the difference is to you between steps 2 and 3. What feels different when you influence the pendulum and when you do not? Each person might answer this differently. Perhaps you feel it in your heart when you are neutral, and feel it in your head when you are controlling the tool. Perhaps you feel more "passive" one way and more "active" the other. There are no right or wrong answers. Only you can figure it out for yourself.

For me, I feel a pressure in my head or in my brain when I am influencing the pendulum. On the other hand, I feel that my mind is more "pulled back" and in neutral when I let the pendulum swing to express its response. Also, if I am thinking Yes or No, then it swings in that direction.

Now you know how to hold your mind in a neutral place. In the future, remember to hold your mind like that when working with the tool in order to obtain accurate answers. Also, if you want to ask about a topic that is emotionally charged for you, take a moment and hold your mind in that place before you ask. The pendulum is most helpful when used without influencing it.

This chapter explained that we can Choose Power by learning how to work with a pendulum to find out answers to questions we have about our bodies and other concerns. Working with a pendulum is an interesting journey. We can learn a lot about ourselves, as well as about our pendulums. They have distinct personalities. For example, it is clear when the pendulum communicates Yes to me, and sometimes it swings so wildly that it is more like Definitely Yes!

Have fun with your new tool.

CHAPTER 4

Power of Attraction

"Plant the seed of desire in your mind
and it forms a nucleus with power
to attract to itself
everything needed for its fulfillment."
- Robert Collier

I have a girlfriend who says she has no luck finding a parking place. She repeats that every time we meet for dinner. On the other hand, I believe that I have "good parking karma." Sure enough, whenever I am looking for a parking place, I find one. We repeat this pattern every time so that I end up driving her back to her car after dinner, because I was able to find a parking place close to the restaurant, and she was not.

What is the difference between the two of us? Am I really luckier than she is? Do I happen to be in the right place at the right time, while she is a couple of seconds too late? Or does the difference have something to do with the fact that I think I have good luck and she thinks she has bad luck?

The Law of Attraction states, "Like Attracts Like." We attract to our lives what we think about the most. Did you ever notice those people who believe they are lucky and continue to win things and date gorgeous people? They attract good things and people, as if they really are as lucky as they say they are.

At the same time, we may know other people who repeat how unlucky and unhealthy they are. They continue to have accidents and health problems. As we will see, it is no mere coincidence that the outcomes matched their expectations.

This chapter explains how we attract people, information and experiences. Once we have a complete understanding about how the Power of Attraction works, then we will be ready to apply the Power of Intention in the following chapter.

Concentrated Energy

Good or bad, what we concentrate our energy on is what we attract into our lives. Repeated daily, we can see, hear and feel how our lives are made up of what we have been attracting.

How do you typically concentrate your energy in your life? Who and what receives your energy? We devote our energy to spouses, children, friends, co-workers and others. Some of us have pets, plants, gardens, classes, volunteer organizations, spiritual groups and so on, which make up our lives.

Although we expend energy on every level, from the spiritual level on down to the physical level, it is most obvious on the physical level. For example, if we spend time and energy with our plants, they thrive. If we do not, they die. This also happens at the emotional level, as the relationships in our lives that are blossoming are thriving because we have put time and energy towards them.

Mentally, repeated thoughts can also Concentrate Energy. Sometimes we concentrate energy by thinking about an event coming up in the future. Have you ever said, "I knew that would happen?" It does not matter if the outcome was good or bad. Concentrating thoughts and feelings around a future event can influence its outcome.

Once, a long time ago, I had a great first date with someone, and it turned into a great relationship. I remember that I kept being afraid that I would "mess it up." Would you believe that I did mess it up and the relationship ended after a very short time? That may have been the first time that I truly realized the power of my thoughts, since the outcome matched the worries that I had about the relationship.

Example - "Computers don't work for me"

Here is an example that I did not fully understand when I first began noticing it. I taught computer classes for years. There would often be one person who came in to the class and said something like, "Computers don't work for me," or "Computers don't like me." Later in the class, his or her computer unexpectedly froze up or did something strange that could not be explained. Meanwhile, other people's computers were behaving just fine. The person who made the statement would look triumphantly at me and say, "See, computers don't work for me." This puzzled me for quite a while.

Gradually, though, I came to understand this to be an example of people attracting what they concentrate their energy on, even if it is not what they truly want. It is the Power of Attraction in action.

Attracting People

One way to notice the Power of Attraction is to look at the people we have gathered around us. Whether we are aware of it or not, we attract and are attracted to people who are like us.

As the Law of Attraction states, "Like Attracts Like," it makes sense to want to have things in common with our friends and family. Whether marital status is important or choice of hobbies (sports or basket-weaving), it is natural to want to be around people who are similar to us.

We often attract and are attracted to people who are in the same situation, or who are mirroring what we are facing. Look around at your friends. What do you have in common with them?

Here is an example. My husband, Mike, tells me stories about how he mirrors his friend, Joe, at work. The two of them have known each other for a long time, and Mike considers Joe one of his closest friends. They were both selected to do the same high-profile job for their company. The similarities did not stop there.

Mike's mom was diagnosed with a terminal illness and died

soon after that. Then, Joe's mom was diagnosed with a terminal illness and died. Mike spent a lot of time dealing with his mom's estate, and then faced significant problems with his siblings who were unhappy with his mother's will. Unfortunately, Joe faced the same issues with regard to his mother's estate and his siblings.

The similarities continue. They both faced major health issues at the same time, and so on. The good aspect of mirroring each other is that they are able to be good support as well as good sounding boards for each other when one of them is going through a hard time. Perhaps this is one reason why the Law of Attraction pulls people together like that.

When We Change Ourselves, We Change the People We Attract

Maybe you have already had the opportunity to notice that when you change, the people in your life also change. You might have noticed that single people tend to hang out with single friends and married people tend to hang out with other couples. I have definitely experienced that in my life as my status changed from being single, to being in a couple, to being single again. When I was dating someone seriously, we would look for other fun couples to be around. As soon as that relationship ended, I ran right back to my single friends so that I could go out dancing with them on Saturday night.

This is a simple example, and it also occurs in other ways. As we change who we are, we change the people who we attract or the people who are attracted to us. I guess that is why relationship coaches say to work on ourselves first.

Attracting People for a Specific Purpose

I remember one time when I was going through a difficult break-up that I became very close friends with two other girlfriends who were also going through difficult break-ups. We really helped each other get through the process of working through our feelings, forgiving the other person and letting go, and moving on with our lives.

It was so interesting to me that when we had all moved on from the break-ups, our close friendships dissolved. Although it seems sad that as soon as we made it through the tough time we did not seem to need each other any more, it also makes a certain kind of universal sense. Maybe we were attracted to each other so that we could be good support and to help each other through the difficult time.

Perhaps you have experienced something like this in your life, too. When our needs change, we change who we attract into our lives. People come into our lives and leave our lives for many reasons.

Reverse Attraction - Letting People Go

I had a friend who I became very close to because she sat near me at work and we both had a lot in common with each other. In fact, we had so much in common that we shared our intimate secrets with each other. Interacting with her was one of the highlights of my work day.

It was a sad day when I realized that she would be moving to a different location to work and I would no longer have the opportunity to see her and chat with her every day. I knew it would be difficult for me. We would be seeing less of each other and probably would not be seeing each other outside of work any more. After all, she had young children and a very different lifestyle from mine. It was no one's fault. The friendship just came to a bit of an ending. Of course, we still have lunch once in a while and keep in touch by email. However, it is not the same close, intense relationship that we shared earlier.

Endings or changes to relationships can be hard to accept. It is natural to go through the grieving process for every ending in our lives. Be patient with yourself. You might feel like crying one day. You might feel extremely angry at that person the next day. There are no right or wrong ways to work through the process of letting someone leave your life. It happens in its own time and in its own way.

The next technique will help you to release any heavy heart energy you have regarding someone who has left your life. Every time you release stored energy, you naturally increase your personal power because the energy is no longer stuck and stagnant. Instead, your energy is free to flow through you and increase your vitality and health.

Technique 1 – Releasing Heavy Heart Energy

Purpose: To work through a relationship that has ended
so you feel better about it.

1) Get into a relaxed state using the Calming Technique described in the first chapter.
2) Think about the person who came into your life and meant something to you. Maybe it was for a short or long period of time. As this person is no longer in your life, take a moment to think about the answers to each of the following questions:
   ~ What caused the relationship to end?
   ~ What did you both have in common?
   ~ Was there something that you needed to learn from the other person?
   ~ Was there something that the other person needed to learn from you?
   ~ What was the purpose of that relationship for you?
3) After the answers have come to you, take a moment to thank the person (in your mind) for what he or she brought into your life. Then, in your mind's eye, watch

---

and feel the person move out of your life.

Open your eyes. How do you feel? Do you feel better about this person than you did before the technique?

If not, please consider some of these recommendations.

Suggestions:
- Do the White Light Technique at the beginning of Chapter 7.
- Do the two Forgiveness Techniques in Chapter 6.
- Do the Power Pose or take a Power Bath, which are presented in Chapter 1.

Attracting Information

In addition to attracting people, the Power of Attraction is evident when we attract information we may have been seeking. Have you ever experienced someone suddenly saying something to you that provides the very answer that you have needed? All of a sudden someone, perhaps even a stranger, tells you something that makes perfect sense to you. Perhaps it is exactly what you needed to hear.

When we remain open to information like this, it can come from anywhere. It might not be a person who transmitted the information. Maybe it is an article in a magazine or a newspaper that has the information that I have been looking for, and I just happened to run across it. I love it when this happens.

My sister told me a story about how she wanted to know where in the Bible she could find her favorite passage. Shortly after, she was watching the Oprah Show, and Oprah just happened to read my sister's favorite verse on the show and then mentioned that it could be found in Psalms. So she got the answer to the question that she had asked in an unexpected way.

Has something like that ever happened to you? I love it when things like that happen unexpectedly. It is comforting to feel that the answers that we need are available to us, using the Power of Attraction. Technique 3 in the next chapter on the Power of Intention can help you to practice this.

Attracting Experiences

Have you noticed the same experience happening to you over and over again with different people or in different places? Maybe you have the same complaint, boyfriend after boyfriend. They all seem to have the same problem. Or maybe similar bad experiences happened in different work environments. For example, the last three of Jane's supervisors have taken credit for her work.

These are also examples of the Law of Attraction. We attract the same experiences over and over again in order to learn a certain lesson.

We will continue to attract the experience until we have learned that lesson. Once we have learned the lesson, the cycle is broken and we will no longer continue to attract the same experience.

Think about it, especially if this has happened to you. This has to be true. How can it possibly be an accident? The mathematical odds of having the same thing happen again and again to the same person are completely against this being a random occurrence.

The Negative Spin Cycle

What are the experiences that you continue to attract? As mentioned earlier, what we concentrate our energies on is what we attract. Good or bad, our lives are made up of where we have been concentrating our energies.

We all have bad things happen in our lives now and then. It may not be anyone's fault. It is just a fact of life that good and bad things happen in life. The question is do we continue to concentrate on bad things, or do we begin to concentrate on good things? It is up to each of us.

People who feel like victims attract experiences that place them in the role of being a victim. If I continue to concentrate on the terrible experiences that have happened to me, then more terrible experiences become attracted to me. It is an energy-draining, self-perpetuating cycle.

I call this the Negative Spin Cycle. The Negative Spin Cycle can be made up of any emotion that makes us feel badly, including anger, guilt, depression, anxiety or jealousy.

If you have watched a friend or family member become "stuck" on one or more negative events happening in his or her life, it is like watching that person going around and around, like clothes in a dryer. Perhaps that person is reliving the same event over and over, telling the same sad story, or making the same complaints about jobs over and over again. I have watched friends and family become stuck in cycles like this.

I have also become stuck in this cycle myself. I have learned the hard way that I am the only person who can save myself and break out of the Negative Spin Cycle. In this way, it is not like a real dryer, where the handle is on the outside. No, in this story, the handle is on the inside and the person inside is the only one who can open the door and leave the cycle. There is really nothing that you or I can do to open the door for someone else. We all need to open our own doors.

Any one of us can easily get caught in the Negative Spin Cycle, going around and around, feeling stuck in negative thoughts. Sometimes I become stuck in a Negative Spin Cycle of guilt. For example, I know that I need to take breaks when I am typing on the computer so that my arms, wrists and back do not become sore. The other day, I was in so much pain because I had been working non-stop at the computer for days without taking many breaks. While my body felt bad, I started scolding myself for this because I "should have known better." I went around and around feeling emotionally badly in this Negative Spin Cycle for a couple of hours before I took the action needed to get out of my cycle of guilt.

The way out is to concentrate on what we DO want. We stop the negative cycle of thoughts by changing the focus from what we do not want and do not like, to what we DO want and DO like. However, the thing that will save us seems like the hardest thing to do, at the time.

Follow the steps in the next technique for a taste of this.

Technique 2 – My Ideal Life

Purpose: To decide who and what you truly want in your life.

Do the following technique when you have plenty of time for self-reflection. Spend time getting to the root of what you would truly like for your life to be like. While writing, follow any detouring roads or trails that appear. Follow them, even if they seem unrelated to the initial question. Have fun!

1) Get into a relaxed state using the Calming Technique described in the first chapter.
2) Take some time to think about each question below, one at a time. Then, write the answers down on paper. Continue to ask yourself:
   What would it look like?
   What would it sound like?
   What would it feel like?
(This includes physical feelings and emotional feelings.)

Then, move on to the next question.

Questions:

What do you want to do in your life?

Who do you want in your life?

What kind of information do you want to attract into your life?

What kind of experiences do you want to attract into your life?

Where do you want to live?

Do you want to travel? If so, where?

What would your life be like if your wildest dreams came true?

What else do you want in your life?

3) Leave the papers from Step 2 alone and undisturbed for at least 24 hours. Then, re-read what you wrote. Is this really what you want in your life? Revise or redo as necessary.

Now that you know what you really want, you can keep these details in the front of your mind. You can think about your answers when your mind is on automatic doing something else.

For example, when you are washing dishes, you can remember some of the places you want to travel. When you are stuck in traffic or at a stoplight, recall some of the other things that you wrote. Think about what you want as often as you can to concentrate mental energy on that.

To summarize, if we start to get pulled into a Negative Spin Cycle, one way out is to replace the current thoughts with thoughts about the people, events and activities we do want in our lives. Here are some additional recommendations for breaking out of the Negative Spin Cycle.

Suggestions:
- Chapter 6 describes techniques such as Immediate Distraction to drive the train of thought to a better place.
- See people, go to the places, or do the things on the Power List created in the first chapter.
- Create a Joyful List in Chapter 6.

We have reviewed the Power of Attraction and how Like Attracts Like in terms of people, information and experiences we attract. We learned that one way to Choose Power is to stop a Negative Spin Cycle by focusing on who and what we want in our lives.

Now that we understand how the Law of Attraction works, how can we use it? The next chapter on the Power of Intention presents some useful ways to bring this idea to life. It also provides the keys to make the dreams unleashed in the last technique come true.

CHAPTER 5

Power of Intention

"You are never given a wish
without being given
the power to make it true.
You may have to work for it, however."
- Richard Bach

The Power of Intention builds on the Power of Attraction and takes it to the next level. The Power of Intention requires more effort than the Power of Attraction. Whether we are aware of our thoughts or not, the Power of Attraction is in process. In contrast, we need to deliberately form an image or goal to activate the Power of Intention. Another way to describe the difference is that the Power of Attraction might feel more passive, and the Power of Intention is more of an active process.

This chapter begins with a story to demonstrate the difference between the Power of Attraction and the Power of Intention. Next, we will understand Creative Visualization and create a Well-Formed Intention. The chapter ends with some ways to practice the Power of Intention.

The Copy Machine that Would Not Work for Me
Although the Power of Attraction works whether you believe it or not, the Power of Intention only works when you believe that it works. This first story demonstrates the difference between the two.

In one of my prior workplaces, there was a man who worked well with equipment, whether it was computers and printers, networks and cables, drills and bits, copy machines, and so on. I was amazed at the way he successfully worked with equipment.

I had a problem with the copy machine. I was convinced that it hated me because it would break down on me very often, especially when I needed to copy both sides of handouts. The machine would stop and the paper would get stuck in multiple places inside, outside and all over the machine. I would go to this man for help, and the machine would respond well for him every time. It was amazing. Did he just have the right touch?

After this happened several times, I started watching how he interacted with equipment more closely. Although he usually swore like a sailor when he was around people, I watched him stroking a computer or machine and talking lovingly to it. When I asked him more about it, he admitted that he believed it was important to talk nicely to equipment.

This surprised me, because this man didn't believe in God, being nice to people, or even eating well. However, he did believe in sending out good energy to machines so that they would work properly.

This is a great example of the Power of Intention. I was exercising the Power of Attraction by expecting that the machine would not cooperate with me, and so it did not. In contrast, he was exercising the Power of Intention by intentionally directing good energy to the machine.

In other words, the Power of Attraction works for everyone, whether they believe in it or not. The Power of Intention is more goal-oriented.

"Deciding Hard Enough"
Here are some more examples of using the Power of Intention. One time when I was between jobs, and conserving my cash, I heard that one of my favorite bands (originally from my home-town) was coming to town. I decided really hard that I would win tickets. My favorite radio station was giving them away all

weekend, and I knew I was going to win!

So, all weekend, I called in to the radio station at the specified times. Finally, it was Sunday night and the concert was the next night. The DJ said he had one last pair of tickets to give away to the person who knew the answer to the question, "Where are the Violent Femmes from?" Of course, I knew the answer! They are from Milwaukee. I called in, I was the lucky caller, I knew the answer, and I won the tickets! I believe it was a result of a strong Power of Intention.

The story continues. In addition to winning tickets to the show, from that day forward I continued to win tickets from that radio station and other radio stations. I could not believe my incredible luck, and neither could my closest friend at the time, because she got to accompany me to a lot of great shows. I got to see the Violent Femmes, Melissa Etheridge, Buddy Guy, Sheryl Crow and many other great performers by being the lucky caller and winning tickets from radio stations. I also won some leather pants, tickets to theater performances and other prizes. It was so exciting because I could continue to enjoy great live music and other prizes without having to pay for them.

I enjoyed my good fortune for about six months. Then, I started feeling guilty about winning so much. All of a sudden, I lost my Golden Touch. I no longer had the magic.

Winning tickets to the first concert was a direct result of the Power of Intention. The feelings of guilt and unworthiness that came later stopped the Power, and stopped the good luck.

Here is another example. I had watched my best friend use a pendulum for years. She could find out answers for people in a couple of seconds about what vitamins, minerals and herbs they needed. It was very impressive to me.

I could not get a pendulum to work for me for years, no matter how much I practiced. Although I worked and worked at it, it would not move for me. I gave up in despair.

One night, I was unable to sleep. I was in failing health and wanted to begin to cleanse my body and start an anti-candida diet. There were so many differing opinions about what foods were best to eat or to avoid on that diet. Plus, different bodies have different needs and different intolerances to foods, as we discussed in Chapter 3.

I was feeling frustrated and desperate. I remember deciding really hard that I was going to make a pendulum work for me that night. The pendulum finally responded to me and told me which foods I needed to stay away from and which foods I could have occasionally and so on.

Whenever I have told either of these two stories to other people, I usually explain that, "I decided really hard and it happened." Have you ever had that experience? Do you remember a time in your life when you wanted something so bad that it was as if you made it happen?

Or maybe you felt as if you were 100% certain that something would occur in the future that you would have bet your life on it? Then it turned out exactly as you knew it would. If you have experienced something like that, then you know what I am talking about.

"A good intention clothes itself with Power."
- Ralph Waldo Emerson

The next sections provide the key ingredients to producing not only a good intention, but a Well-Formed Intention. We will also explore how to use this in combination with emotional energy to produce desired results. Some people refer to this process as Creative Visualization.

Creative Visualization
These are fancy words to describe what we do whenever we imagine the future before it happens. The only difference is that with Creative Visualization we send a deliberate intention and

imagine good things happening. We use the same time and energy that we might spend worrying about something, and instead think about what we really want to happen.

One key to a successful intention is to use your senses as much as possible. See the pictures of your desired future in your mind with vivid colors and other specific details. Hear the voices and words that you want to hear. Feel the feelings that you want to feel. We will discuss all of this in great detail in this chapter.

I have used Creative Visualization many times in my life before speaking to a high-profile group. The night before, I would sit and get into a relaxed state using the Calming Technique described in the first chapter. Then, I would imagine myself in the situation the next day. I imagined it going very well. I saw the people there, and I heard someone telling me that I did a great job. I felt happy and proud that I did the best that I could have done.

After each presentation, I was very happy with how the speaking event went. I don't think it was a mere coincidence.

It was an example of using Creative Visualization, which is simply taking time to apply a Well-formed Intention and to see, hear and feel the results that we want in our minds. Before we discuss Well-Formed Intentions and Emotional Elements, here are some more examples illustrating the Power of Intention in the context of dating.

Dating Example One

Once I had a friend who announced in early May that she needed to find herself a summer fling. The next time I saw her, she was with a drop-dead gorgeous man and looking very happy. He had a boat and they spent a lot of time together that summer. When the summer was over, we were discussing men and she complained that this man didn't seem to be serious about her, and didn't seem to be taking the relationship seriously. I reminded her of her intention that she announced at the beginning of the summer that she wanted to find a summer fling. I congratulated her that she got exactly what she wanted.

She didn't seem to recognize her Power, and instead looked rather sad and depressed. This is one example to demonstrate that we get what we ask for.

Conclusion: Be careful what you ask for, because you might get it!

Dating Example Two

Being specific is important. I have another friend who sent out an intention on New Year's Eve to find a man who she could commit to for the rest of her life. She got all dressed up, and went to a party that would have good potential for her to meet someone single. Sure enough, she found someone interesting. One thing led to another, and they ended up in bed together that evening.

Long story short, the man did not become her Mr Right. However, my friend became pregnant and therefore got her own man who she could commit to for the rest of her life. She had not expected that the result of her intention would be her son!

Conclusion: Be specific with your intentions!

Dating Example Three

After I had been dating for a number of years, I decided that I was ready to send out an intention for a steady boyfriend who I could spend time with regularly on the weekends. However, I wanted to have the weekdays to myself to keep up with my friends, and do the countless activities, plays, parties, happy hours and other events that single women do.

Sure enough, shortly after sending out the intention, I started to date someone for a significant length of time. It started out to be exactly what I wanted.

After a year, I began to realize that he did not ever call me during the week. Didn't he ever think about me during the week, I asked him tearfully? "Couples usually want to see more of each other, not less," I complained. Regardless of what he said, I knew that what I had pointed out was true.

Finally, one day, I realized that I had received the exact relationship that I had requested. Consequently, I changed my intention and asked that this relationship turn into something more committed. I sent the intention out several times. Although he did propose and we began to look for a house to buy together, the relationship ended up falling apart.

Conclusion: Strange things can happen when you change an intention.

Like me, you may suddenly realize that you received exactly what you asked for with your original intention. In other words, you may realize that you made a mistake or forgot some detail that now seems very important. If so, then stop, and start over with a new intention. Before you do that, review what you received. Use it as feedback, so that next time you know what to change about your intention. The next example will make this clearer.

Dating Example Four

During my last major break-up, I was devastated because it was unexpected and there was apparently no room for negotiation or discussion. To pull myself out of the cloud of self-pity, and a major depression that threatened to drown me in my own tears at times, I sent out an intention that, "I would find such a great partner that all of my previous relationships (including this one) would pale by comparison." I loved that phrase: "pale by comparison."

It wasn't easy, I admit that freely. It does take incredible effort to change thinking in the middle of a crisis and get out of the

Negative Spin Cycle. Chapter 6 provides more techniques about how to do that.

Whenever I was able to do this and pull myself out of the fog of depression, I could experience a break in the clouds. The sun poked its head out for a moment to remind me that it was not the end of the world, there were other fish in the sea, good could come out of bad, every cloud has a silver lining, etc. You know all those things that well-meaning people say.

I followed up on the intention to find a great partner by writing a list of everything that was important for me to have in my ideal partner. The list continued to grow, and ultimately became four pages long. When I shared my idea of this list with some of my girlfriends, they would roll their eyes and say, "You will never find a man to meet all of your requirements."

I knew for certain, deep down, that I would find the man with everything on the list because I had successfully attracted relationships using the Power of Intention before, as in Dating Example Number Three above.

I knew that I have consistently received exactly what I have requested. In fact, I used my recent break-up as a cue to review the problems in that relationship and to learn from them. On my new list, I made sure to add those important details that were obviously missing from my first list, so that I could avoid repeating the same problems in my next relationship.

As a result, I did receive EXACTLY what I asked for and found the man who met all my requirements on the list! We are still together and have gotten married. So, I know the importance of being specific. I remain convinced that making a list and sending out a Creative Visualization works every time.

Conclusion: Review what you received. Use that as feedback and adjust the specific details next time you use the Power of Intention, so that it is more accurate regarding what you really want to receive.

Summary

To review, the important points to remember from these stories are:

1) Be careful what you ask for, because you might get it!
2) Be specific with your intentions.
3) Strange things can happen when you change an intention.
4) Review what you received. Use that as feedback and adjust the specific details next time, so it is more accurate regarding what you really want to receive.

Well-Formed Intention

A Well-Formed Intention is the key to a successful Creative Visualization. A Well-Formed Intention is a statement that is very clear and easy to understand. Keep the following important points in mind.

First, it is important to frame things in the positive. Saying things like "I don't want to feel pain," or "My pain will end," does not work, because the mind has to create the pain and then erase it. The result of this intention would be continued pain. Another bad example is saying, "I want a man who isn't jealous." It backfires because the mind picks up on the jealous and delivers that.

To prove this to you: Don't think of a banana.

Well, can you?

Your mind works to conjure up the image and then works to erase it. That is not an effective way to use the mind. It is so much better and more efficient to phrase the intention in terms of what you DO want in your life.

For example: Think of an elephant. Is that easier to do than to "not think" about a banana? This example explains why it is better to ask directly for what you DO want instead of focusing on what you DO NOT want.

The examples above can easily be transformed into Well-

Informed Intentions, such as, "I want my back to feel good and strong," and "I want a man who trusts me completely." These messages are clear, direct and can be easily packaged up and delivered into my life. This is often as easy as dropping the negative and choosing a phrase that means the opposite.

Second, it is important to choose something that 100 per cent of you wants. If you are at all divided about it, then rethink your intention. For example, if one part of you really wants the job that you interviewed for, and another part of you does not want to do the same type of work any more, requesting the job using a Well-Formed Intention will not work well for you. Similarly, the intention also has to be consistent with your morals and values, or it will not deliver the desired results.

Third, a Well-Formed Intention is one which you believe you can achieve. Can you really see yourself running a marathon? If you can, then this is a Well-Formed Intention.

Also, the intention needs to focus on you. Attempting to change someone else's thoughts, feelings or behaviors sets us up for failure.

Finally, the intention has to be something that you feel you deserve. If this is not true, it will not work for you.

Here is an example of a simple intention that I did. For one job, I was asked at the last minute to find some vendors to sponsor our conference at $500 apiece. It was six weeks until the conference, and my supervisors did not expect that I would find any vendors who would agree to participate with such short notice. Regardless, I sent out an intention that I would find 12 vendors to sponsor our conference.

Six weeks later, everyone was astounded. I had found a great group of vendors and they were all very excited to be there and paying us $500 apiece. The total number was not 10 or 13. When the results were in, I had found exactly 12 vendors to help us to fund the conference, which exactly matched my intention!

Technique 1 – Creating a Well-Formed Intention

Purpose: To write a list of the specific details that you want.

Follow these two steps to design a Well-Formed Intention for something you want. It might be a partner, a job, a house, loyal friends or something else. Include all of the details that are important to you.

1) Create a Well-Formed Intention that meets all of the requirements listed above.
2) Take the time to make a list and include all important specific details.

I recommend writing down specific details on paper, especially the first time that you do this. Although this is not necessary, I have experienced much better results when I take the time to write the details down on paper.

Writing down intentions is helpful for many reasons and in many ways. First, it makes us take the time to actually sit down and ask ourselves what we really want. Second, we can be as specific as we can be. Third, it becomes more real in our minds when we see the details written out. Fourth, we can easily review it and modify it as needed. Finally, we can quickly read it several times a week and keep it in the forefront of our minds.

If you think of anything important that you do not want, then remember the importance of phrasing all the details in the positive, as previously explained. Any negative statement can be turned into a positive statement by simply removing the negative word and turning the statement to its opposite.

Once you have the Well-Formed Intention and specific details written down, keep the list readily available so that you can continue to add to it or modify it as you think about it over the next couple of weeks.

It is a good idea to review it once a day. Then, you can put it away until the next day.

Emotional Element

For a successful Creative Visualization, it is important to attach an emotion to your Well-Formed Intention. People who are successful at producing outcomes like I did with the vendors in the last story say that it is important to feel what it would feel like to have the outcome already. So, in addition to imagining it in our minds, we need to feel the Emotional Element in our bodies, as if to convince ourselves that we already have it or that it has already happened.

As we will learn in the next chapter, the mind and the emotions are linked. They need to stay linked when using a Well-Formed Intention in a successful Creative Visualization. So, feel that feeling as strong as you can in your body. Some of you might be very good at this. For those of you who need to practice this, the questions in Step 4 of the next technique are very helpful.

Technique 2 – Creative Visualization

Purpose: How to manifest an outcome using an Emotional Element.

This technique leads us through the process of visualizing a specific upcoming event. Read it through ahead of time so that you are prepared.

1. Before you begin, take some time to think about what you want to happen at the event. What would be the best outcomes that you can think of for this event? Be specific. Listing them on paper, as in the previous technique, can be helpful when you get to Step 4.

2. Get into a relaxed state using the Calming Technique described in the first chapter.

3. Think ahead to a situation that you know is going to happen. This might be a meeting, a presentation or other group event. Picture the scene happening in your mind right now. For example, who is sitting and who is standing? Take the time to picture as many details as you can. Feel what the temperature might feel like. Whose voices do you hear? We are "setting the stage" for the action to occur in the next step.

4. Now that you feel that you are in the scene, you are ready to change the picture so that you see and hear your specific outcomes that you listed above in Step 1 occurring. See your outcomes happen in your mind. What does the picture look like, as your outcomes unfold? Hear other people responding to you. Focus on how you will be feeling when your outcomes happen. Feel that feeling now. How would you describe the feeling? Where do you feel it in your body? Does it feel like it is moving or still? If it feels like it is moving, how is it moving and where is it moving? What shape is the feeling?

5. Once you are able to locate and feel the feeling in your body, now imagine what it would feel like if you could

double that feeling. Feel it being twice as strong as it was in Step 4.

After the event has occurred and is behind you, then take some time to review how well your intended outcomes matched the actual outcomes. How did it work for you? Did your outcomes manifest as you imagined they would? What details did you overlook? What would you do different next time? You might want to take notes about what worked well while the feedback is fresh in your mind.

Now that you have designed a Well-Formed Intention and done a simple visualization, do you feel how powerful you are? Do the two techniques back-to-back about the same topic for added power. Once you have been successful on a small scale, you will have the confidence to apply these techniques to any area in your life. Take on new challenges to improve your skills. The potential to create your life is unlimited.

Keep in mind that a successful Creative Visualization requires a Well-Formed Intention and an Emotional Element so that the mind and body stay linked. This is a great recipe for success.

My hope is that you find many ways to apply this power in your life. To help you get started, I have supplied some stories below, and then three sample ways to apply the Power of Intention in your life.

Samples and Examples

My sister recalled her story about meeting Harrison Ford. She had heard that he would be attending an event in her hometown. Two weeks before he came, she wrote down her Well-Formed Intention that she was going to meet him face-to-face and shake his hand.

It turned out that she was catering a party that he attended. She kept an eye on him while she was working. Although he had been surrounded by people, suddenly he was standing alone. She approached him and said that she really admired him and would love to shake his hand, and he did. She told me that she believed this was all a direct result of her Power of Intention. She reported that she was on Cloud Nine for the whole night, and that she did wash her hand eventually!

Here is another story that happened before I learned to make a list of qualities I wanted in a love relationship. I remember that I used to think that I would not be able to get everything that I wanted in one man. I did not think I could find someone who matched me on every level: intellectually, emotionally, spiritually, socially and sexually. I figured that no one was perfect and that I would have to give up one of these qualities.

I decided that if I had to do without one of those aspects, then I would choose to give up the emotional aspect. I thought that I would be able to fill my emotional needs with my girlfriends and my family. Sure enough, the next man who I dated did not show any emotions and only wanted to see me every two weeks or so because he was afraid to get any closer than that.

Luckily, I later convinced myself that I could get everything I wanted in one person. I could have it all! I sent out the intention that there was a man who was the perfect match for me on every level and would meet all of my needs.

Consequently, I am now with a man who is the perfect match for me on every level. I would not have found him if I had not changed my thinking. In other words, I would still be with imperfect men if hadn't believed there was a perfect man out there for me.

Another way that I use the Power of Intention is while I am driving. When I want to change lanes into a lane of traffic that is full of cars, I send out an intention that there will be a space for me to merge into traffic. I love it when the space appears, and it does every time, even in heavy traffic.

How else can you play with this power that is so responsive to intentional thought patterns? Continue to brainstorm about ways to apply the Power of Intention in your life.

The remainder of the chapter presents three sample ways to practice applying this power. These are great opportunities to expand your skills. I encourage you to design your own, too.

The first example allows us to practice attracting something specific. For example, can we attract information that we need whenever we choose? Test out the next technique to find out.

Technique 3 – Deliberate Intentions

Purpose: To practice attracting something specific to you.

Follow these steps to send out a Deliberate Intention. You might start with something simple. For example, you might request an answer to a specific question that you have been pondering lately. Or you might practice attracting a good referral to a doctor, or hair stylist, or mechanic or someone else that you need.

1) Create a Well-Formed Intention that meets all of the criteria listed in that section above. For example, do you feel that you deserve it? If not, pick something that you feel worthy of having. As mentioned, it will not work for you unless you feel that you deserve it.
2) Get into a relaxed state using the Calming Technique described in the first chapter.
3) Do the Power Pose, as described in the first chapter.
4) Say your Well-Formed intention out loud or to yourself.
5) Do a Creative Visualization from the previous technique

---

to increase your success.

Repeat this once a day for a week to get the answer or referral. Be open to receiving the information from anywhere or anyone in your everyday life. For example, it might come from a good friend, a stranger on the bus, an article in the newspaper or some other source that might not have been the one you expected.

Bending Time

Have you ever had the experience of being at an event that seemed to have lasted longer than it actually did? The event might have been a party or a wedding or a day at the amusement park. Perhaps you were on vacation and the experience is very memorable to you.

When you think about the event now, you might remember it with very vivid colors, or it might feel like it lasted a long time. This is an example of bending time.

On the other hand, when we are waiting in a long line, or sitting in a dentist's chair listening to that awful high-pitched drill, time seems to slow down. At those times it would be helpful to know how to speed up the experience of time. We can speed up or slow down time whenever we choose, simply by applying the power of our intention.

To speed up our experience of time, we can do things that we enjoy doing. Do you know the saying, "Time flies when you are having fun?" Therefore, have as much fun as you can! Read a book while waiting in line. Chat with other people in line with you.

I also have a technique that I have been using in the dentist chair for years. I close my eyes and think about a beautiful place that I have visited. Usually I pick Hawaii, so I go to Maui in my

Mind. I remember the beautiful beaches and rolling waves. I see the eerie fog when we drove up the volcano. I relive the snorkeling and the colorful fish we saw, and so on.

I bring the experiences back to life in my mind by seeing what I saw, hearing what I heard and feeling what I felt. Whatever is happening in my mouth seems to be less noticeable and to fade into the background. It definitely makes getting my teeth worked on so much more pleasurable and it is like watching home movies!

On the other hand, sometimes slowing down time is desired. Maybe you are in a long-distance relationship and the weekends are your only time to spend with your loved one. While receiving a massage or taking a vacation, it is fun to slow down time so the experience seems to go on forever. I love it when I come back from a week's vacation and I feel like I have been gone a month. The next technique provides steps to slow down time so that joyful moments can be savored and feel like they have lasted a nice, long time.

Technique 4 – Slowing Down Time

Purpose: To be aware of everything simultaneously.

The secret to slowing down time is to experience everything going on around you at the same time. These steps can help.

1) It is most important to set the intention first. Before or during the event, take a couple of minutes, STOP, and state your Well-Formed Intention. Intend something like, "I want to slow down my experience of time today by noticing everything I can at the same time."
2) Pay attention to everything at once. Feel the cool breeze

---

on your skin, experience the warmth of the sun on your skin, notice the people around or the butterflies flying by, fall into your lover's eyes completely, and so on. In other words, be as completely in the here and now as you can be. Do not think about the past; do not worry about the future. Keep bringing yourself back to the present.

3) Continue to answer these questions:

How many different senses can I pay attention to simultaneously?

What do I see, hear, smell, taste?

What feelings do I feel?

Where do I feel those feelings in my body?

How many different sounds or conversations do I hear?

4) Repeat Steps 2 and 3 as often as you can to stay in the present.

Later on, when you look back on your experience, you will notice that you have forged great memories and the event will seem to have lasted longer than it actually did. Even if you were only at the event for a few hours, it may have felt like you spent a longer amount of time there.

Starting Something

> "If you employed study, thinking,
> and planning time daily,
> you could develop and use the power
> that can change the course of your destiny."
> - W. Clement Stone

It is most fun to use the Power of Intention to start something that we feel passionate about. That way, we can feel how powerful we are, and have fun at the same time.

For example, my mother decided that she wanted to start a Psychic Fair in her community. She organized and recruited readers, vendors and volunteers. She secured the location and hung flyers to advertise it. And she did all this without any training or an MBA. It was a smashing success and is now an annual event.

Here is another example. When I was single, I could have spent my time complaining to other women about the quality of men. I could have felt depressed day after day, week after week, because I had not found my perfect partner. Instead of reacting in ways like this that would perpetuate a Negative Spin Cycle, I took advantage of every opportunity to meet single men. I remained hopeful and focused on my Well-Formed Intention, described earlier. I also decided to throw a Singles' Party for my community.

I was intrigued by an idea I saw on television, in which single women brought single men who they were not interested in to a party together. I was inspired to throw a party like that. I created some great interactive games in which people would need to talk with strangers in order to play the games. My friend agreed to let me use his awesome house, and I invited people from several different singles lists. I promised a prize for the person who invited the most single people to the party.

Although I had not thrown a party like this before, I had wanted some of my single female friends to meet my single male friends. People loved the games, had a great time and the party was a wonderful success. One couple met there, started dating and eventually got married. They are still together. I had originally thought it was just something I wanted to get out of my system once, but due to numerous requests, I ended up organizing several more parties. Many matches were made.

The point is to capitalize on the Power of Intention by starting something new that we are passionate about. Something happens when we follow a dream or start living our passion. Suddenly, we attract people that want to help us, and other magical things happen.

To summarize, the Power of Attraction explains how we attract people, information and experiences to us. The Power of Intention builds on that by allowing us to Choose Power to deliberately change who and what we attract into our lives.

Perhaps you are aware of the Power of Attraction and the Power of Intention, and still have not experienced the results you desire. The next chapter will address the subtleties of the mind that can cause even Well-Formed Intentions to get off track.

CHAPTER 6

Power of the Mind and the Emotions

"Knowing others is intelligence;
knowing yourself is true wisdom.
Mastering others is strength;
mastering yourself is true power."
- Lao Tzu

Sara just got into a terrible argument with her friend on the phone. It would be easy to feel badly and revisit the fight in her mind all day long. Or she can direct her mind some place else. She could choose to stop focusing on her bad feelings from the fight, and start focusing on something positive instead.

Maybe she is going to a party tonight. She can set an intention to meet an interesting and exciting new person at this party, and Concentrate Energy on that possibility. Now, she feels good, and is excited and happy, instead of feeling sad or angry or guilty.

As we continue to practice the Power of Attraction and the Power of Intention, we realize that the mind is a powerful tool. Thoughts and feelings constantly come and go, like weather, through the mind. Which thoughts and feelings do we hang on to, and which ones can we easily release?

Chapter 4 explained how it is easy to get caught in a Negative Spin Cycle made up of fear, depression, jealousy, resentment, guilt or something else. Although it may feel like we are trapped in a spiral of negative feelings, we can Choose Power and change this emotional turmoil of the mind at any time.

Our repeated thoughts and feelings create us and our lives. They do this by attracting more experiences that mirror our emotions. When we feel good, we attract more to make us feel good. When we gain control of our thoughts and feelings, we can feel good more often and attract more of what we truly want into our lives.

This chapter discusses ways to control the emotional energy of the mind. First, we will learn Mind Keys to use with our emotions. Next, we will practice Immediate Distraction, create a personalized Joyful List and explore some ways to change our perspective. Finally, we will learn techniques to stop negative thinking, to forgive, to enhance good memories and to take the "juice" or "kick" out of bad memories.

Keys to the Mind

We begin with the shifting nature of emotions. Our emotions can shift and change quickly and frequently throughout each day.

Although Virginia may wake up feeling good, if she spills her coffee and has to change her clothes, she can become angry at herself. This bad feeling can ruin her entire day, if she lets it.

On the other hand, Thad might have been upset from missing the bus, when suddenly his new girlfriend calls him. This pleasantly surprises him. Now, he is smiling broadly, and nothing else seems to matter.

I like to compare emotions to the weather. Have you ever heard the saying, "If you don't like the weather, wait five minutes?" The nature of the mind and emotions resembles nature itself. The weather comes and it goes. Clouds come, and clouds go. Rain showers come and rain showers go. Thoughts and emotions are the same way; they come and go just as easily.

Perhaps you have not thought about emotions like this before. Think about this idea, now and then. Perhaps every time that you see a cloud, you will be reminded about how thoughts and emotions come and go. Although they may feel just as unpredictable as the weather, the three Keys to the Mind provide the secrets to control the emotions.

Since emotions shift easily and frequently, we can learn to shift our emotions toward the positive end of the spectrum whenever we realize that we are feeling bad. When we are feeling good (happy, content, loving), our minds can attract good things. When we realize that we are feeling depressed, angry, or jealous, we can remind ourselves to shift that energy and get back to feeling good.

That was just the three Mind Keys in a nutshell. Think about them as keys to unlock the power of the mind. Let's take the Mind Keys one by one.

Mind Key #1 is to monitor our emotions and take our emotional "temperature." Simply stop, check in and ask, "How am I feeling right now?" When I take a moment to stop and check in with my current emotional state, I have done a powerful thing. At that moment, I have the power to change the emotion that I am experiencing.

Ask yourself the question, "How am I feeling right now?" Although it can be helpful to pick a name for the emotion (angry, sad, happy), good or bad also works fine. If the answer is good, or happy or joyful, that is great. If the answer is bad, then continue with Mind Keys #2 and #3, which are explained in this chapter.

Conclusion: Mind Key #1 is to take our emotional temperatures. How am I feeling right now?

Why Grief is Important

It is okay to discover that I am feeling badly. All of us experience painful events in our lives. People die. Jobs end. Friends leave our lives. We experience health problems. It is natural to react to stressful events with negative feelings.

Grief is one common emotion that we feel naturally in response to endings. Since I have mentioned the importance of grief and grieving at different times in this book, let's address it in greater detail now.

Grieving is an important process that we all go through, whether we want to or not. Many levels are involved when we work through our different feelings and reactions.

The mind, the body and the spirit help us to face and endure stressful events, like endings. The mind may need to look at an ending from different perspectives. The body, too, needs to express emotional energy in its own way so that it does not get stuck in our bodies, and turn into health problems later. If I feel sad, it is natural for the body to want to express the sad energy by crying, for example. Spiritual questions may also come up that we need to answer for ourselves.

Did you know that we also grieve when good things happen to us? Even when we are excited about an upcoming change, certain things may come to an end, and so it is natural to grieve for what will be missed. For example, when Claire got a new job that paid better and was closer to her home, she was really excited. At the same time, she also knew she would miss seeing her current co-workers and some of her clients.

Another example is a couple with a new baby. Although they are very excited that their dream has come true, certain things in their lives have also come to an end. Whether it is hobbies, habits, the career track, social life, spiritual pursuits, personal freedom, or something else, it is best to let the mind and body grieve for what has ended.

Therefore, even if we do not fully understand what our minds or bodies are doing, it is important to let them help us to come to terms with endings and other challenging events that happen to us in our lives.

For example, if you feel like crying and have no idea why, then cry. It is healing to let the body express the emotion of the moment, especially if you are alone and can take a moment for yourself. Just like the weather, the emotion will pass.

Feeling the Emotion, Then Letting It Go

The point here is not to avoid feeling bad emotions, such as grief. It is important to fully feel and experience your current emotion, whatever it is, in the body. This is how we process the natural endings and other unpleasant experiences that happen in our lives.

It is like letting the feeling wash over you like an ocean wave. Imagine that you are in the ocean and you see a big wave coming at you and you cannot get out of the way in time. Prepare yourself for the wave, then let it wash over you. It is not so bad and will pass, quicker than you might think.

The point is that after fully experiencing a negative emotion, let the feeling go. Let the feeling move on, and replace it with another feeling. Spilled coffee first thing in the morning does not need to ruin the entire day.

Therefore, Mind Key #2 involves two big steps:

1) To identify and feel the emotion, and
2) To let negative feelings go.

Some of us are better at one of the steps than the other. The next technique helps us to practice both.

Technique 1 – Feeling the Emotion, Then Letting it Go

Purpose: To become good at identifying and feeling the emotion, and then letting negative feelings go.

We will fully embrace the emotion of the moment, and then release it, to move away from us. This technique works well for both minor frustrations like missing the bus and for major challenges like the death of someone close.

Use it any time you feel bad. Add any personal details to

---

the technique to make it more enjoyable.

1) Get into a relaxed state using the Calming Technique described in the first chapter.

2) When you feel ready, think about the situation that is causing you grief. Review the event or situation in your head. Feel the accompanying emotion. Is it sadness, loss, anger, betrayal, guilt or something else? Pick out a name for it.

   Allow the feeling to wash over you. Give yourself over to the feeling. If you have not done this before, simply test it out.

   You will discover that you are fine, even though it might seem like a scary notion. Give yourself permission to express the feeling. It is all right to cry, scream, laugh or throw things at the wall (not at people).

   Know that the feeling will not destroy you. It will pass.

3) Stay with the feeling as long as you need to feel it. After you have been with the feeling, you will notice that it is no longer as strong and intense as it was. The energy of the feeling will seem to peak, and then lose its "juice" or its "kick." It is no longer so intense.

   This is the time to tell the feeling, "Thank you for the gift that you brought. I now release you and allow you to move on." Watch and feel the feeling move on away from you.

4) After you have done Step 3, ask yourself whether you still feel connected to that feeling. If you do, then imagine the strings or ropes that show that you are still connected to the feeling. Now, see great big scissors

appear in your mind's eye. Watch them cut the strings so that the feeling is free to move away from you. Feel free to blow some air at it to get the feeling to begin to move away from you. Watch and feel the feeling move away from you until it is so far in the distance that you cannot see it anymore.

5) When you are finished, do something completely different. Immerse yourself in a book or movie. Call up a friend or family member and discuss something besides this topic. Do something that feels good.

You are training your mind that it is all right to experience the emotion, and then to let it go. You are also learning how to be in control of your mind and emotions.

Once you work through this technique, you will know that an emotion has no power over you. You will have proof that you control your emotions; they do not control you. You can release feelings whenever you choose.

It is very important to fully experience all emotions, even the negative ones, so that they do not become "stuck" in the body. Then, let negative emotions go. Processing emotions like this helps the body to release them.

If you are facing a major life event, like the death of someone close to you, you might notice that the negative feeling returns to you again and again throughout the day. Every time that you realize that it is back, greet it like a friend. "Oh, I know you. I see that you are back." You may need to repeat the technique several times a day at first. Repeat it as often as needed. I repeated the same steps listed above several times daily and over the course of several weeks after a bad break-up.

Note: Regarding Step 3, the length of time to stay with

the feeling before it weakens will vary from person to person, from situation to situation and even from day to day regarding the same issue.

The first time that you do the technique and let the emotion wash over you, it will probably feel the most intense for you. The next times that you do it, the feeling may be less intense. Of course, feelings also recur. For example, on the anniversary of a death, someone might have the most intense feeling that he or she has ever felt about the loss.

Know in your heart that whatever happens is normal. A wide range of responses are possible, and everyone processes things differently. Please be patient and gentle with yourself.

I know from my own traumatic experiences that I often thought the negative feelings hung around longer than they ought to. I started thinking, "I should be over this by now." Luckily, I have wise and supportive friends who disagreed with me and continued to remind me that it could take longer than I want it to take.

You do have the strength to get through this experience. If you keep doing this technique, the negative feeling(s) will get less intense and will visit you less often. Depending on your specific situation, one or more of these recommendations might help.

Suggestions:
- Do the Power Pose or take a Power Bath, from Chapter 1.
- Do something on your Power List, created in Chapter 1, or your Joyful List, designed later in this chapter.
- Practice Immediate Distraction, as described later in this

chapter.
- The Minimizing Bad Memories Technique later in this chapter can take the "juice" out of a bad memory.
- The two Forgiveness Techniques later in the chapter can also help, if needed.

Conclusion: Mind Key #2 is to fully feel the emotion. Then, let negative emotions go.

To summarize so far, we have learned that Mind Key #1 is to stop and check in with ourselves about how we are feeling. If the answer is good, that is fantastic. If we find ourselves feeling bad, then Mind Key #2 is to feel the emotion, and then let it go.

It is important to understand that we choose how to feel at all times. We are not at the mercy of emotions. No one else can make us feel a certain way and we cannot make someone else feel a certain way.

Feelings come from within, so my feelings are entirely under my control. The next story illustrates that principle.

Thoughts Lead Emotions

"Between stimulus and response,
there is a space.
In that space lies our freedom
and power to choose our response.
In our response lies our growth and freedom."
- Viktor Frankl

Victor Frankl wrote about surviving a Nazi concentration camp in *Man's Search for Meaning*. He explained that even in the midst of this terrible situation, he still had the power to choose his attitude.

He could choose for himself whether he was going to react with despair and hopelessness about his situation, or with hope and love.

He noticed people in the same life-and-death situation reacted differently. One prisoner might have the attitude that, "it is no use," and give up, stay in bed and die. Another person might choose an attitude of compassion, and donate portions of food so that another needier person might have more.

The author explained that even though they controlled almost everything, the captors could not control his attitude or his determination to survive. If he was able to hold on to his power to choose his attitude in those terrible circumstances, we have the power to do the same in our lives.

Maybe we are unhappy with our job. As Victor Frankl says, we have "the power to choose our response." We still do possess the power to choose to be hopeful and believe that better opportunities exist out there for us.

A small shift in attitude means the difference between feeling badly and feeling good. Although the same tragic life event could happen to two different people, each could react differently. For example, take two people who have just lost their jobs. One person might take it personally and dwell in self-pity for weeks, while the other might focus on the new opportunities that are out there. The difference depends on their trains of thought.

It is important to understand that the mind and the emotions are linked. Specifically, thoughts lead the emotions like a train engine controls the movement of the caboose. Where one goes, the other follows.

When we think negative thoughts, the emotions follow and we feel badly. When we think positive thoughts, we feel good.

We can use the same amount of energy to think about good thoughts, rather than dwelling on the negative. For example, if I dislike my job and find myself complaining about it, I can use the same energy I would use complaining to look for other job opportunities instead. At the very least, I remember that I am not trapped, and that I can leave my current troublesome situation at any time. At most, I might find something that I am really excited about and change my life completely.

The previous technique, Feeling the Emotion, Then Letting It Go works well for processing specific life events. Once we have processed an emotion, we can let it go whenever we choose.

The next technique is not for specific life events. Rather, it is helpful for people who experience negative thinking in certain places, such as driving to work, or in bed at night. The technique can be done anywhere because we will imagine ourselves in those places.

Technique 2 – Stopping the Negative Thinking

Purpose: To teach the mind to control the thinking
process.

If you have negative thinking that plagues you when you are alone, or going to sleep, or driving in your car or some place else, it may leave you feeling badly. The next technique provides steps to stop yourself from thinking about certain trains of thought in a specific location.

1) Get into a relaxed state using the Calming Technique described in the first chapter. Pick a safe place where you will not be disturbed.
2) Imagine yourself in the place where you experienced negative thinking. Where were you? What were you doing when you started thinking about this? Were you driving, lying in bed, taking a bath? Imagine yourself there now (driving, lying in bed, taking a bath, etc).

Remember the details of your surroundings as accurately as possible until you feel like you are actually there.

3) Now, instead of letting the train of thought continue, see and hear yourself saying, "Stop." Then, imagine yourself standing up and doing something completely different to interrupt your train of thought. (If you were imagining yourself driving, first imagine yourself pulling over, stopping the car and then doing something else.) If you cannot think of something else to do, then imagine yourself clapping your hands or turning around in a circle or doing something else that effectively interrupts the mind.

4) Now, repeat this for other places where this happens. For example, I know people who review their days in their mind when they are in bed, which interferes with their sleep. If this happens to you, hear and see yourself saying, "Stop." Then, imagine interrupting yourself and doing something else instead of allowing your mind to continue.

Repeat for other places, if applicable.

5) When you are finished, open your eyes. Immediately do something else. Play your favorite CD or DVD. Make a cup of tea. Call someone and talk about something else. Read a book. Go for a walk. Sing a song.

In the future, when you are in the same place that you imagined yourself in the technique, you will now be more likely to remember to interrupt thoughts when you start negative thinking. This technique teaches the mind to control the emotions by interrupting negative trains of thought.

Suggestions:
- To work through a relationship that has ended, do the Releasing Heavy Heart Energy Technique in Chapter 4.
- The memory techniques later in this chapter can help to decrease the emotional effects of a negative memory.

Switching Trains of Thought

Mind Key #1 is to check in and take our emotional temperatures. Rate the current emotional state. How am I feeling? Good or Bad?

Mind Key #2 is to feel the emotion. Then, let negative emotions go.

Mind Key #3 is to switch our trains of thought. We can replace a thought with another at any time. It is as easy as thinking about something else. We can either take the same train of thought to positive perspectives, or we can switch to a completely different, positive train of thought.

The point is to think about something positive so that the emotions follow, like the caboose, and now we feel emotionally good. Although people, places and events that make us feel badly exist in life, there are also people, places and events that make us feel good. We constantly choose where to focus our attention.

For example, when I see dark clouds outside my window instead of sunshine, I feel disappointed. However, I can change my train of thought, and say, "This is a great opportunity to stay in and read a book / clean my house / watch this movie." Change the focus to a positive thought and it changes how we feel.

Here is another example. Often after I have taught a class, I think back on the one thing that did not go quite as well as it could have, and think about what I could have done differently, instead of focusing on everything that went well. It is just as easy for me to drive my train of thought to focus on the positive as it is to focus on the negative.

Therefore, use Mind Key #3 to replace negative trains of thought with positive trains of thought. Who and what makes you happy? We can transform our lives by regularly using this simple process, because our trains of thought drive our behavior and our emotions.

Remember Sara from the beginning of the chapter? She could have thought about the terrible fight with her friend all day long. However, she chose to get off the train of thought involving her friend, and get on a new train of thought that involved the upcoming party. Since the emotions followed the train of thought, she felt happy and excited as a result, instead of feeling depressed.

Every time that the fight crossed her mind, she could send some loving energy to her friend using the White Light Technique at the beginning of Chapter 7. Then she could use Immediate Distraction (below) to shift her mind to another subject, such as the party, so that her emotions follow and she feels better.

Although the following techniques to switch our trains of thought are simple, they may not be easy at first. Often, it seems easier for us to dwell on the bad parts of our lives, and complain to others, because everyone else is doing it. It takes more effort to take control, and drive the train where we want it to go. However, it is worth the effort.

"That which we persist in doing
becomes easier for us to do
not that the nature of the thing itself is changed,
but that our power to do it is increased."
- Ralph Waldo Emerson

Everything becomes easier with practice. In this case, too, it becomes easier to replace our trains of thought. The mind learns to respond to our guidance, and our lives feel more pleasant more of the time.

Immediate Distraction

I like to use Immediate Distraction to choose a different attitude because it works quickly. If I focus my mind on something specific that takes mental energy, then I can stop obsessing about a topic gnawing away at my brain. For example, when our brains are busy concentrating on something like a crossword puzzle, we cannot keep thinking about break-ups, or money problems or anything else.

Here is another example. When I worked at a job I strongly disliked, it would have been easy to think about my job and feel depressed and powerless all night long. The better choice, however, was to crawl into bed with a good book. This was a successful solution because I could not dwell on my job, and read at the same time.

I also enrolled in dance classes and Spanish classes. These worked well because they started right after work and I could not think about my job while I was counting dance steps or learning another language.

I felt so much better after doing these activities because my mind had a break from thinking about my job. It was better to be thinking about my classes than feeling depressed and powerless.

I like to watch the movie, *The Secret*, whenever I am feeling down. The movie is one of my favorite Immediate Distractions. It reminds me that I create my own life. Both the book and the movie are extremely inspiring, and I recommend them highly. When the movie ends, I feel better.

Do you have any movies that leave you feeling happy or inspired? What can you do right now that will make you smile? Who can you call or visit who makes you laugh? These are good examples of doing things that make you feel good.

The next technique will assist us in creating our own, personalized Joyful Lists. Once created, we can use them anytime in the future when we are feeling low. We can pick something on the list to do that feels good and is an Immediate Distraction for the mind.

In other words, we can effectively choose Joy as the current emotion at any time by doing something on the list. Remember, wherever the thoughts go, the emotions and behavior follow.

Technique 3 – Joyful Lists

Purpose: To create a Joyful List that you can use for Immediate Distraction at any time.

In this technique, you will brainstorm about all of the people, places, memories, events, activities and other things that bring you joy. Once you create this personalized list, you will be able to pick something from your list to immediately shift your attitude from a negative one (depressed, angry, resentful or irritated) to a positive one (optimistic, joyful, content, loving or peaceful).

List as many items as you can on the following pages (or in your own notebook) that bring you joy. The suggestions below may help you to get started. Once you are finished you will have a list of activities that can change your attitude at a moment's notice so that you can choose joy.

Although you might get ideas from some of the questions below, free your mind to recall other people, events and experiences that bring you true joy. After all, you know yourself best.

Here are some questions to help you to begin.

~ What songs will instantly put a smile on your face?

Write them down or better yet, create a CD for yourself of all of these songs so you can play it whenever you choose.

~ Does singing your favorite songs bring you joy?

~ Who do you know in your life who can cheer you up when you are in the middle of a challenging situation? List your supportive friends or family members.

~ People who can make you laugh are invaluable. Spend time with these people. Maybe someone's child brings you joy when you spend time with him or her.

~ What memories do you have that put a smile on your face? My memories of Hawaii and Cozumel instantly do that for me. I go to these places in my mind when I am in the dentist chair or the chiropractor's office. Make a list of your favorite memories.

~ What movies or television shows are upbeat and cheer you up? Dr Norman Cousins describes in his book, *Anatomy of an Illness*, how he healed himself of a life-threatening disease by watching funny shows like the "Three Stooges" and Marx Brother movies.

~ Are there places where you can go that make you happy? Hiking out in nature brings me a sense of peace. Does it have that effect on you?

~ Do you have a pet that brings you joy?

~ What activities can you DO right now that will bring you joy? For example, ride your bike, play with your dog, lie out in the sun, kiss your honey, read a good book, take a Power Bath (see Chapter 1), dance to your favorite song, work in your garden, bake cookies, write a poem, get a massage, go to the gym, and so on.

~ How has the Calming Technique or your own personal meditation practice been working for you? Does it instantly shift your mood? The Calming Technique now does that for me. Feelings of bliss can replace a negative feeling such as anger or depression.

I know someone in Narcotics Anonymous who uses meditation to replace drugs in his life. Whenever he has a craving, he sits down to feel the Blissful Moments described in Chapter 1. Apparently, this good feeling feels just as pleasant as his former drug.

~ Do you do yoga? I remember in the 1980s when I first began to take yoga classes, I told people that it was almost as good as sex, because my whole body felt exhilarated afterwards and my mind was completely at peace. Is there anything like that for you?

~ What else makes you happy? Do you love to shop? Do you love to dress up and go out? Or, on the other hand, do you prefer to spend your Saturday nights at home reading? Do you spend time at the arcade, or on the internet (listservs, blogs, wikis, gaming or other social networking sites)? Include anything that brings you joy.

My Joyful List

Spend time with these people/children:

Think about these memories:

Listen to these songs:

Go to these places:

Watch these movies:

Do these activities:

Other:

Conclusion: Mind Key #3 is to switch the train of thought to topics that feel good. Immediate Distraction and using your Joyful List are examples of this.

Summary of Mind Keys
To review, here are the Mind Keys:
- Mind Key #1 is to take our emotional temperatures. How am I feeling?
- Mind Key #2 is to feel the emotion. Then, let negative emotions go.
- Mind Key #3 is to switch the train of thought to topics that feel good.

Follow these steps on a daily basis. This recipe can transform your life. It also helps during traumatic life events like deaths, break-ups or the end of a job. For major life events such as these, you might find yourself following these steps several times in one day. The next day, you might not need to do them at all. Pay attention to your own needs and respond accordingly.

People who experience frequent anxiety and depression may choose to consult with health professionals, as therapy or other treatments might help. However, practicing the steps above repeatedly can also help you learn to direct your mind away from some subjects, and toward others.

You can learn to be in control of your thoughts and emotions at any time. Test it out for yourself and be convinced that this is true:

"Nothing external to you has any power over you."
- Ralph Waldo Emerson

We learned that driving a train of thought to a joyful thought can make us feel better because emotions follow thoughts like the caboose follows the train engine. Using Immediate Distraction and Joyful Lists are great examples of Mind Key #3; other ways are to change perspectives.

Have you ever noticed that when you leave town, you can think about your life differently? Situations look different; relationships feel different. New ideas appear out of nowhere, or the answer to a problem may become obvious.

These are examples of results that can occur when we change our perspectives or viewpoints. In addition to leaving town, other techniques to change how we view our lives include the Bird's Eye View and volunteering in our communities.

Bird's Eye View
The following techniques are all under the category I call Bird's

Eye View because they allow us to see our lives from a different point of view. A bird flying high over your neighborhood sees your back yard differently than you do when you look out your back window. In the same way, we can see the situations in our lives differently when we are not so emotionally close to them. I have provided three different variations on this technique, so choose the one(s) you prefer.

One approach is to imagine yourself floating above your body so that you see your situation from miles above in your mind's eye. Have you ever looked at a map on the internet and "zoomed out?" It is like moving higher in the sky away from the map. The picture appears different now; the perspective has changed. Do that with your issue so that you can see yourself in the picture. How does that change the way you see your situation? How does it change the way you think about it?

A second approach is to ask the question, "Will this matter to me 20 years from now?" Imagine that you are 20 years in the future, looking back at your life now. This is another way to "zoom out" and see your situation from a more objective point of view.

A third approach is to discuss your problem with someone who can see your situation from a more objective point of view. Other people have a Bird's-Eye View of your life. Because of this, other people can sometimes see the solutions to your problems, and give you answers you need because they are not blinded by your blind spots. Be sure to ask the other person to keep the information private, if that is important to you.

Volunteer

Another way to change perspectives is to volunteer to help a charity or organization. Doing this helps us to feel our power immediately and in so many different ways because of the great feedback. Often when volunteering, we will find ourselves helping people who are worse off than we are. This opens our eyes quickly to how blessed we are. We feel gratitude for what we do have. Suddenly the world looks and feels differently than it did before we began to volunteer.

Maybe you are not receiving the recognition or appreciation that you feel you deserve at work or at home. When you volunteer your time, people often go out of their way to thank you for helping out. This is a great way to feel connected to people, feel appreciated for your time and feel your personal power.

Perhaps you feel that what you are currently being paid to do is not meaningful. I felt that way when I was a cocktail waitress. What great service did I perform when people could just go to the bar to get their own drinks?

Building houses for Habitat for Humanity or recording books for the Blind and Dyslexic feels directly meaningful because it helps someone else. It is great to feel like we are making a difference in the world.

Choose from the range of volunteer groups that exist to find the one that fits with your interests or skills. Groups exist to help the arts, nature, children, the elderly, the homeless, the hungry, those who cannot read and more. Maybe you have a preference for a specific group of people who you want to help.

Or perhaps your skills will drive your choice. If you like to build and work with your hands, then Habitat for Humanity might be the best fit for you. If you enjoy television programs about courts and lawyers, perhaps you would like to start the process of becoming a court-appointed advocate for abused children.

If you do not have any children of your own, and would like to have one in your life, Big Brothers, Big Sisters might interest you. If you like plays, local theater companies love to find volunteer ushers who can hand out programs in exchange for seeing the play for free. If art is more in line with your interests, check in with local art galleries which may be looking for volunteer tour guides, or docents. In any case, volunteer if you have not, to feel your personal power and to change your perspective immediately.

To summarize, when we stop and check in with ourselves and realize that we are feeling badly, we have several options. They all involve driving the train of thought down certain tracks so that the emotions follow, and we feel better. Some examples that we explored included taking a trip, seeing it from a Bird's Eye View and volunteering in our communities.

Another way to change perspectives is through forgiveness. If you find yourself bothered by unhappy memories from your past when you do Mind Key #1, the rest of this chapter addresses forgiveness and other ways to enhance memories.

Forgiving and Enhancing the Past

If we spend time and energy remembering what someone said or did in the past that continues to bother us, we might feel badly today as a result. Luckily, we have the option to practice forgiveness which allows us to heal.

Forgiving another person does not help the other person; it helps us. The other person may not even be aware that we hold something against him or her; however, we know that we do and so it is really hurting us. Reliving a negative experience from the past brings it to the front of our minds so that we feel badly in the present. Even though the situation may have happened 20 years ago, we are still feeling badly now.

Negative feelings pull power away that could be used in a more productive way to enhance our lives. Therefore, forgiving someone else helps us because we can transform the bad memories and bad feelings into peace and wisdom.

If you would prefer to confront the other person and get it out "on the table" with the possibility of clearing the air, then the communication techniques at the beginning of Chapter 2 will help towards that goal. If, on the other hand, you prefer not to deal with the other person at all and to work through forgiveness on your own, then the following two techniques allow healing without the other person's assistance or participation at all.

Technique 4 – Positive Intentions Behind the Behavior

Purpose: To prepare to truly forgive someone.

In this technique, you will "step into another person's shoes" in order to understand their position. The goal is to discover the positive intention behind the person's words or actions.

1) Get into a relaxed state using the Calming Technique described in the first chapter.
2) Pretend that you are in a movie theater, watching yourself and the other person(s) on the screen. Watch the entire story that needs forgiveness on this screen, from beginning to end. Remember that you are not looking out of your eyes in the memory on the screen. Move out of your body so that you are sitting in the movie theater watching yourself and the other person(s) on the screen as the memory unfolds.
3) After you have watched and listened to the entire story, imagine yourself stepping inside the other person.
4) In your mind, ask that other person what his or her positive intention was behind this behavior. What might have been that person's reason for acting that way? Clear your mind and wait for an answer to come to you.
   After an answer has come to you, ask whether there might be another positive intention behind this

---

behavior. Continue to do this, until you stop receiving answers.

5) Repeat Steps 3 and 4 only if there are other people involved in this event that need to be forgiven.

The knowledge we gain from this technique is often enough to help shift our energy that is stuck; it allows the forgiveness to flow. Often we find that the person acted out of some self-centered interest or to help someone else.

This information is helpful because we realize that the other person is only human and not perfect. Also, we realize that the person did not do this in order to hurt us. This tends to be an eye-opening experience.

Perhaps now you feel released from this incident and are ready to forgive this person and let the memory go so it no longer bothers you. Forgiveness is a powerful tool that can relieve burdens that you have been carrying.

You will know that you have been successful when you think about the person or the memory. Although you might still be aware of sad or bittersweet emotions, you will feel a shift so that you feel freer, and maybe lighter, as if a load has been taken off of you.

If you do not feel that you are quite there yet, you might still need to express thoughts and/or feelings about the situation before you can truly let it go. If that is true, the next technique helps to unload the thoughts and feelings that may have been stored up inside for a significant length of time. Once these are released, forgiveness becomes easier to do.

Technique 5 – Writing the Letter that You Will Not Send

Purpose: To release strong thoughts and feelings you have about someone to make room for forgiveness.

This technique works well when you want to say something to a person, and you know that it will only make the situation worse. I have done this technique several times in my life to let different people go, and have found it to be highly effective in every case.

1) Get into a relaxed state using the Calming Technique described in the first chapter.
2) Write a letter to the person. Include everything you would like to say to that person that would help you to express the thoughts and feelings that you may have been carrying for a long time. Continue to edit the letter until you release all of the thoughts and feelings from your head and your heart.
3) When you are finished, destroy the letter using one or more of the following techniques:
   ~ Tear up the letter in many little pieces.
   ~ Light a fire in your fireplace and toss the letter in. Watch it burn.
   ~ Bury the letter in your garden or another appropriate place.

This technique works so well and I cannot explain why that is. Perhaps these are words that we have wanted to say to that person for years, and now the words have finally been expressed. Perhaps, now that we have expressed our truth, we feel better and are now ready to let it all go as we watch the letter being destroyed.

Regardless of the reason that it works, it does work and the energy is no longer stuck inside. Those of us who have done this technique know that destroying the letter is often the best approach. In the end, it is not really important that the other person read the letter that you have written.

However, after completing this technique, some people have chosen to send the letter, and I believe that each of us makes the best decisions available to us. Think this through, before you do, though.

Although writing the letter may have helped you to feel better, the other person will not experience the letter in the same way that you did. If you decide to send the letter, be prepared for the possibility that the other person may become defensive and may focus on the mistakes and faults in your letter. Therefore, be open to the outcome going either way, positively or negatively. In other words, it could make matters worse, or make them better.

Suggestions:
- The White Light technique from Chapter 7 is a nice way to end this technique.
- If you skipped the previous technique, Positive Intentions behind the Behavior, it can help you to forgive someone.
- Take a Power Bath or do something on your Power List, both from Chapter 1.

Forgiveness allows us to release the thoughts and feelings surrounding a negative memory that may have disturbed us for years. There is no need to condone the other person's behavior or to bring that person back into your life. The only point is to release the energy that had been bottled up inside of us for so long. Now the energy is freed up to improve our lives instead of being stuck on a past situation.

The remainder of this chapter addresses ways to improve other memories from the past. For example, we can enhance the good memories that we have.

Power from Memories

Memories and stories are important because they made us exactly who we are today. I know people who like to share stories and memories from their past with me regularly over dinner. Both positive and negative events brought us wisdom that we might not have learned any other way.

Memories that we are reviewing in our minds also lead our trains of thought down certain tracks and result in very predictable emotions. When dwelling on bad memories, the body responds as if the bad memory is happening again, right now. By reliving the memory, we keep our body feeling anxious and upset which causes stress and illness.

Many studies have confirmed that our bodies react to an imagined event the same way that they respond to an event that actually happens. To prove it to yourself, stop and close your eyes and imagine that you are sucking on a lemon. Do it, now.

Isn't it fascinating that your lips start to pucker, even though no real lemons are around you?

This is an example of how memories become alive to us, here and now. Just as the memory of the lemon tightens our lips, bad memories cause us to tense up. However, there is a technique to take the "juice" out of bad memories so that they have less of a "kick."

On the other hand, we can use this to our advantage for good memories. How do we make them seem more alive, in the here and now? The secret is to notice which position we are in when we "see" our memories in our minds.

There are two different positions in our memories. We either remember from inside our bodies or from outside our bodies. Close your eyes and think of a memory. Do you see the memory occurring from your own eyes, inside your body? Or, are you outside your body in the memory and looking at yourself, like looking at a picture of you?

We remember memories both ways and each has its own advantages for different purposes. When we remember from within the body, then we feel the emotions of the memory stronger.

When we remember from outside our bodies, the emotions are removed. Therefore, it is best to look out of our own eyes while remembering good memories to enhance the good feelings. On the other hand, it is best to watch ourselves from outside of the body for bad memories so the power from negative feelings is removed.

For some reason, though, we tend to remember memories the opposite way, even though the bad memories seem more painful that way, and good memories are not as powerful as they could be.

The next two techniques will help to enhance our good memories, and take the "juice" or the "kick" out of bad memories. They are fun and quick to do.

Technique 6 – Enhancing Good Memories

Purpose: To remember positive experiences through our own eyes.

1) Get into a relaxed state using the Calming Technique described in the first chapter.
2) Close your eyes and recall a pleasant memory.
3) When you look around in the memory, do you see yourself in the picture or are you looking out from your eyes and remembering it as if you were reliving it again?
4) If you can see yourself in the picture, then change it so that you are actually in your body, looking out from your own eyes. In your mind's eye, step into your body. Relive the experience again from this perspective. Remember what it looked like. What did people say or what other sounds did you hear? What smells or tastes do you notice? What did it feel like?
5) When you are done, open your eyes. Clap your hands or stand up and turn in a circle or get a cup of tea. This breaks your mind state.

   Now think about your experience again. Does it seem more intense, more positive and more memorable? Now, and in the future, whenever you think about this memory again, it will have this added positive charge.

Do this to other positive memories that you want to enhance.

Technique 7 – Minimizing Bad Memories

Purpose: To remember negative experiences from outside
the body.

If you have a bad memory that is haunting you, here is one
way to stop it from having power over you.

1) Get into a relaxed state using the Calming Technique
   described in the first chapter.
2) Recall a bad memory. Do not choose something very
   traumatic the first time through this technique. Choose
   something minor, such as something that happened at
   work. Close your eyes and remember what happened.
3) When you look around in the memory, are you looking
   out from your eyes and remembering it as if you were
   reliving it again? Or, do you see yourself in the picture?
4) If in your memory you are looking out from your own
   eyes, then change it so that you float up and out of your
   body and are now looking down on yourself, seeing
   yourself in the picture. Watch and listen to the entire
   experience again from the perspective of being outside
   your body.
5) When you are done, open your eyes. Clap your hands or
   stand up and turn in a circle or get a cup of tea. This
   breaks your mind state. Now think about your
   experience again. Does it seem like it has lost its
   emotional charge? Now, and in the future, whenever
   you think about that memory again, it will have lost its
   "juice." That is because you can be more objective and
   feel less intense emotions about it when you remember
   from outside the body.

Repeat this technique with other negative memories to minimize their power.

Once you have worked through these techniques with specific memories, you will notice that the memories stay that way for you. The good memories remain enhanced, and the bad memories lose their emotional power over you.

This chapter offered a wealth of techniques for Choosing Power with the mind and emotions. The three Mind Keys allow us to drive trains of thought to positive places and feel good. We can do this with Immediate Distraction, using our Joyful lists, and by changing our perspectives. Forgiveness and enhancing our memories can also transform our lives.

The next chapter discusses Spiritual Power. We will discuss how love and gratitude are the cornerstones of a powerful life.

CHAPTER 7

Spiritual Power

"I have learned through bitter experience
the one supreme lesson to conserve my anger,
and as heat conserved is transmitted into energy,
even so our anger controlled
can be transmitted into a power
that can move the world."
- Gandhi

I used to supervise an employee who had a bad attitude. She complained about everything and did as little work as possible.

I did the White Light Technique (presented later in this chapter) for her, and was very surprised at the transformation that happened. In a very short time, she became a model employee. She became extremely pleasant, completed a lot more work and volunteered for new assignments. No one could believe the transformation that had taken place with her.

We have seen from the chapters in this book that we can Choose Power in many different areas in our lives. We have explored Power from our Bodies, Power with People, and the Power of our Mind and Emotions.

We now turn to the Spiritual Power behind many religious traditions. The White Light Technique is an example of using Spiritual Power.

This chapter explains how the Power of Love can transform our lives by redirecting energy. After that, we will discuss the Power of Gratitude and Self Gratitude.

The Power of Love

Have you ever been in love with someone? Remember how everything about life seems much better? I notice the beautiful flowers and the blue sky, and I tend to smile more. I wake in the morning thinking about my beloved and easily start the day feeling good. This is a great way to feel the Power of Love.

The Power of Love is often said to be the source of life on our planet. In our lives, we may find it easy to feel love with our family and friends. We feel loving when other people help us out, and when we help out other people, such as when we give money and gifts to needy families at Christmas.

Other times, it is not so easy to feel loving. Love does not seem to flow as easily when it comes to difficult people in our personal and professional lives. When someone does something stupid in traffic, I do not feel loving. When another person has hurt my feelings, it is often hard to be honest and let the other person know. So, some conflicts do not get fixed. I know that I have walked away from friendships instead of having the difficult conversations that might have resolved the issues that drove a wedge between us.

The Power of Love can help us with difficult people and difficult events in our lives. First, we will review how we usually see conflicts played out in the movies and in everyday life. Then, I will explain how Redirecting Energy can help two opposing forces find a solution.

In the Movies

In most movies, we can easily spot "the bad guy." He is usually dressed in black and has a moustache. We know who "the good guy" is because he is wearing white. Conflicts are oversimplified in the movies like this because one person is right, and the other person is clearly wrong. We like black-and-white conflicts like this, because they make conflict seem so simple. Since we have seen movies for years, we might think that every conflict has one person who is good and right, and the other one who is bad and wrong.

Although conflict is usually presented simply in the movies, conflicts are more complicated in real life. It is not so easy to label one person "good" and the other "bad." What if both people in the story are good people? What if both people are right?

In fact, both people are right, in their own minds. They are also right in the stories that they are telling to other people about the problem. We all spend time and energy developing our side of the story so that we can persuade others that we are right. This is because we buy into the belief that one person is right and the other wrong, and deep down we want others to tell us that we are right.

Ongoing Struggle Causes Ongoing Struggle

When each person works to rally more people around their side of the story, it is hard for the love to flow. The opponents are focused on proving to other people that they are right, instead of spending time and energy to find a solution that could make everyone happy. In addition, each keeps looking for more evidence to support their story that the other person is a bad person.

The next quote also explains ongoing struggle.

"What you resist persists."
- Carl Jung

With regard to the Law of Attraction, this also means that "resisting" will result in attracting more to resist. "Resisting" can mean complaining about what someone did or something that happened. The important key here is that I know when I am in this "resisting" attitude because I am critical and focused on the negative. If I continue to resist people or events in my life, I attract more people and events in my life to resist.

The Undo Key

I am reminded about a short story that I wrote years ago called "The Undo Key." As a computer trainer, I taught how pressing the Control-Z keys made the computer Undo the last action.

In my short story, the character wanted an Undo Key for her life after she endured a bad break-up, as a result of saying the wrong thing at the wrong time. She thought, if only she could press an Undo Key, she could Undo the conversation that led to the break-up.

Well, as much as we might like to change or Undo something that has already happened, we cannot. We are wasting our time and energy if this is our goal. In addition, we are resisting the current situation.

For example, if I get into a car accident, does it help to start wishing that it did not happen? Although I can complain to other people as much as I choose, it will not change the fact that I got into a car accident. It is a better use of time and energy to fix the problem, rather than to complain about someone or something that happened.

The Words We Use

Perhaps you have noticed that a lot of the words and language that we use also implies resisting, such as, "I am 'fighting' this cold," "there is a 'war' on drugs," "we are 'fighting' crime," etc. The examples go on and on, and I'm sure you can think of many more. The words imply a stand-off, in which two opponents have locked their horns in direct opposition to each other's goals, and are participating in an ongoing struggle. If we continue to use words that suggest ongoing and unending struggle, then that is what we will continue to experience in our lives.

Here is another explanation of ongoing struggle:

"Every action has an equal but opposite reaction."
- Sir Isaac Newton

A good example of this Third Law of Physics is that if I push against you, you push back with the same amount of force. We can see this push-back from opposing forces played out in our society in so many ways: wars, crackdowns on violence, management against staff, landlords against renters, Pro-Choice versus Pro-Life, Democrats against Republicans. When one person takes an action against another and the second person resists, their energies can cancel out each other's actions.

If this is true, how can we ever get anywhere or make any real progress?

Redirecting the Energy

Instead of continuing to push against our opponents, a better response is to Redirect Energy into something better. This approach of Choosing Power is to rise above the conflict using the Power of Love.

Here is a picture for you. Imagine two cars driving towards each other on the same road. There is a long bridge between them that only has room for one car at a time. Since neither car wanted to wait, now they are both in the middle of the one-lane bridge and no one wants to back up. Neither car can move forward because the other one is blocking progress. How do the two people find a solution to their conflict when they are blocking each other like this?

If both are unwilling to move back, the only way to go is up. This is metaphorically where we will find the solutions for many conflicts. Redirect the Energy that was in opposition towards Love and Spiritual Power instead.

The way out of conflict is to accept that both people are right and they are both good people. This idea is not brand new. If you have already read Chapter 2, recall how the phrases, "You're Right," and "I Agree," helped to shift the energy in conversations. When two people have been pushing against one another, if one stops pushing, the other one also has to either stop pushing or fall forward.

OK, since we cannot really fly up into the air, how do we Redirect Energy in everyday life? Here are some recommendations.

Drop the need to be right. Remember that all sides have truth. Send out a simple intention to rise above personal differences and focus on similarities and solutions. Expect the solution to appear, according to your spiritual beliefs, and it usually does. Then, everything shifts and this shift makes all the difference.

Previously, the focus and energy would be on opposing the other person and telling the story to friends and family. Now, the focus can be on finding a solution so that everyone's needs are addressed.

As long as there is a positive intention to shift toward the Power of Love, the energy will shift from the negative to the positive. You will know when you have shifted in this direction because you will feel it inside yourself. You might feel like you are suddenly smiling on the inside about the other person or the other group.

This is the true Power of Love in action. Now there is freedom to focus time and energy on finding a good solution to the problem.

My partner does this very effectively with me when I lose my temper and start to complain. He Redirects the Energy by simply smiling back at me. He does not "push back" at me with an equally bad temper. This is so effective because once I have said what I needed to say, then I start smiling, too.

I recommend this Smiling Technique. You might practice it the next time someone is "pushing your buttons." It works wonders!

Since our society does not regularly practice or promote this Redirecting Energy approach, this may be a new idea to many of us. Let's take a look at some more examples to better understand how this can work.

Judo

One great example of Redirecting Energy is judo. This martial art teaches techniques that use an attacker's aggressive action so that the energy works against the attacker.

For example, if someone lunges at me, I can apply a subtle technique that turns him a bit, and his initial energy continues to move him forward, past me. He lands on the ground behind me, causing me no harm.

Notice in this example how I would not stop or block the attacker's initial energy because that would cause pain or injury. Rather, judo takes the energy that is coming toward me and Redirects the Energy so no harm comes to me. This is the key to the Power of Love: to Redirect the Energy so it causes no more harm.

Mahatma Gandhi and Martin Luther King Jr

Additional examples of Redirecting Energy are the nonviolent approaches used by Mahatma Gandhi and Martin Luther King Jr. Both leaders were convinced that this approach was the most potent weapon available to help oppressed people to gain their freedom.

These two powerful leaders put the Power of Love into action by responding to violent actions with nonviolent reactions. Gandhi used this approach to help win India's independence from Britain. During the Civil Rights movement in the United States, Martin Luther King Jr promoted non-violent means to achieve civil-rights and was awarded the 1964 Nobel Peace Prize. Their life stories prove that the Power of Love can produce incredible changes in the world.

These leaders chose to use nonviolent resistance because it leaves no bitterness in the opposing group. To avoid the usual, predictable results I described earlier in this chapter, these leaders wanted solutions that would avoid causing ongoing struggle and violence with the group who had been oppressing them. Instead, they Redirected their Energy upward and rose above the conflict to find new answers and actions.

Like Gandhi and Martin Luther King, we might transform other people's lives when we use this transforming Power of Love. However, even if our actions do not affect anyone else, Redirecting Energy helps the one that practices it.

Our thoughts are now on creative transformation and compassion, and no longer on struggle or confrontation. Because our thoughts change, we now feel good. This approach frees us so that we can rise above the struggle of opposing energies.

Love Attracts Love

As explained in Chapter 4, Like Attracts Like. Similarly, Love Attracts Love. As you practice expressing love in your life, you will naturally attract more loving people and positive events into your life. Approaching the world from this point of view changes everything. It brings completely new choices that we have not seen before. How can you apply this principle in your world?

One way I like to practice the Power of Love is to use the White Light Technique to heal a relationship. My sister first introduced it to our family years ago. It is such a simple technique and it seems to work for any situation. I have already referred to it several times in this book, because it is one of my very favorite techniques.

This approach cannot make a situation worse; it can only help to improve a relationship with a particular person in your life. You might do it for someone who seems difficult or troublesome to you, or for someone who you love deeply. In any case, this transforms a personal or professional relationship by directing positive energy towards the person.

It has worked for me every time that I have done it. Repeat it over a period of time to improve any situation with another person. The results are amazing!

Technique 1 – White Light Technique

Purpose: To improve your relationship with someone.

1) Find a quiet place where you will not be disturbed. Get into a relaxed state using the Calming Technique as described in the first chapter.
2) Close your eyes and visualize the person. Then, in your mind, see that person being surrounded by white light. The white light represents love and positive energy. Hold the image as long as you can.

The beauty of the technique is in the simplicity of it. The longer that your sessions last and the more often that you do this technique, the quicker you will notice concrete, positive results in your relationship with this person.

As I mentioned at the beginning of the chapter, the first time I used it was with a difficult employee who I was supervising. My mother suggested that I do it. In a very short time, the employee's behavior shifted completely. She became much more pleasant to work with and transformed into a model employee.

The next time I used it with a difficult supervisor who did not like me and treated me badly. After I did the technique consistently over a period of time, her behavior completely shifted, too, and she started being much nicer to me.

My friend, Mary, suggested substituting yellow roses for the white light, especially if you need to forgive the person, or if that person needs help to forgive himself or herself. As long as you are expressing love towards this person, feel free to transform the technique in any way that makes sense to you and your religious and spiritual beliefs.

The White Light Technique is a great way to practice the Power of Love in your life. It brings positive energy into any relationship, and the other person will not know what you did unless you tell that person.

Another way to practice Redirecting Energy is to do the Mirror Instinct Technique. It can help you to rise above the situation or conflict, and also to figure out why you are having difficulty with a certain person.

Mirror Instinct Technique

This technique also helps us to practice the Power of Love. We tend to attract people that mirror us so that we can learn about ourselves. Although it is often hard to be objective about ourselves, we can usually be objective about other people and see them more critically. That is why other people's faults appear very obvious to us, and we often have blind spots about our own faults.

Here is how the Mirror Instinct Technique works: if I have a specific criticism of someone else, it is because I have the same criticism about myself. If I stop and ask myself how this criticism applies to me, sometimes, it is like a curtain being pulled back and I can see it from a completely new perspective.

For example, I have been secretly amused when I have witnessed disagreements between people, and Person A is accusing Person B of something that Person A does frequently. Of course I can see it, because it is not my blind spot. Although I can see other people's blind spots, I cannot see it when I am accusing someone else of doing something that I also do.

Here is a great visual explanation. Perhaps you have heard the saying, "when you point a finger at someone, there are three fingers pointing back at you."

Test it out right now. Look at your hand when you point at someone as if you are scolding him or her. Notice the other three fingers are curled back towards you.

Tone of Voice example

Here is an example of how I used this. One of my biggest issues with a former supervisor was the tone of voice she used with me. It really bothered me. I would describe it to others that she talked to me like I was a dog.

Although she didn't use this tone of voice every time, when she did, I could rarely stay in a conversation with her for very long. The tone of voice seemed to imply that she was frustrated with me, that I was stupid to be saying what I was saying, or asking what I was asking. It felt like I was bothering her when she could be doing something else that was more interesting or more important. All of these details are really important and will be useful later in the story.

Whenever she used that tone of voice on me, I usually ended the conversation as soon as I could. At times, it also kept me from approaching her for the next couple of days so that I would not need to experience it again.

One day, out of the blue, I got off the phone with a customer service representative who I considered to be inept and ineffi-cient. That night, I kept thinking about the conversation and hearing bits of it being played back in my head and I realized that I was left with a really bad feeling about the experience. In fact, every time I thought about it, the bad feeling returned. I slowly realized why that conversation bothered me. It was **my** tone of voice that bothered me. It felt as if someone else had used it with me, instead of me using it with someone else.

This was the insight that I needed. Just like my complaints about my supervisor, I realized that sometimes I use a tone of voice on the phone when I am feeling impatient, or like I am wasting my time when I could be doing something more important. (Notice how this is all repeated from above.) I learned that it is my own tone of voice that bothers me when I use it on others, and I feel like someone used that tone of voice on me.

This revelation is an example of how to use the Mirror Instinct Technique to work for us instead of against us. I experience someone else's behavior as an issue or a "pet peeve" and when I dig deeply, I discover how I do the same thing, and how it secretly bothers me.

This has freed me up in my relationship, too. I realized that I had resisted getting into a serious relationship because so many couples I know use a similar disrespectful tone of voice with each other. I heard that tone of voice a lot while I was growing up, and so it would be easy for me to repeat this behavior in my own relationship.

Because of this tremendous insight and link back to my own behavior, I am more conscious about the tone of voice that I use with my partner. Just because he loves me deeply, does not justify me speaking to him in a disrespectful tone of voice indicating that I am impatient, or he is stupid or I could be doing something more important.

The Mirror Instinct Technique has helped me in several other interpersonal situations. In this example, I was able to get to the root of one pet peeve which I thought had nothing to do with me, and everything to do with my supervisor. Finding out the truth set me free.

Technique 2 – Mirror Instinct or "Pet Peeve" Technique

Purpose: To get to the root of understanding why someone else's behavior bothers us.

This technique requires some inner work. Pick a time when you know that you will not be disturbed so that you can get to the core and the truth for yourself.

---

1) Find a quiet place and get into a relaxed state using the Calming Technique described in the first chapter.

2) Think about a pet peeve. Write down what bothers you the most about it. Use these questions to help prompt your mind.

   ~ Describe the pet peeve in as much detail as you can. What is your experience of it?

   ~ Use sensory terms. What does it look like, sound like, feel like, smell like, taste like?

   ~ Use a story to compare your pet peeve to something related. Does your pet peeve remind you of something else? Can you think of a metaphor for it?

   ~ What bothers you the most about it?

   ~ Does it bother you in all situations or only during specific times?

   ~ Does it ever NOT bother you? If so, when?

3) After you are done, still in your quiet space ask yourself the following questions.

   ~ Has someone else ever said the same thing about me?

   ~ How can this criticism also apply to me? (Perhaps it only appears in specific situations.)

4) At times, the answers will come immediately. If so, forgive yourself for the behavior. Then, congratulate yourself for getting to the bottom of the difficulty. Once you have discovered the real root of the difficulty, it is like the blinders have been taken off, and it has less power over you.

5) If no answer appears, be patient. Answers may not come immediately. Send out an intention such as, "I want to find out why this bothers me so much so that I can be free of it." Hold the intention in the back of your mind over the next week. Stay open to new ideas that might

come to you. A good example might occur to you over the next couple of days. You might see a movie or something else might happen that reveals the answer. Perhaps someone may make a comment that shows how the situation can be applied to you.

Once we know how a pet peeve applies to us, it no longer has the strength and intensity it once had. Perhaps we are more forgiving about it now, so it bothers us less to notice it in other people. It is like our blind spot used to have unconscious control over us, and now we are free.

Remember, if you ever feel stuck, discussing it with a trained therapist can help. One or more of the following might also offer relief.

Suggestions:
- Immediate Distraction (from Chapter 6) works well as a complement to this technique.
- Do something on your Power List (Chapter 1) or Joyful List (Chapter 6).
- Take a Power Bath or do the Power Pose (Chapter 1).

Power of Gratitude

Another way to Redirect Energy and rise above an issue is to use the Power of Gratitude. As in the Power of Attraction, in which Like Attracts Like, feeling consistent gratitude attracts more to our lives for which to be grateful. Here is a great example of the tangible results produced from expressing gratitude.

Dr Masaru Emoto conducted pioneering work by showing written words to water samples and then crystallizing them. He demonstrated that the human mind changes the way that crystals grow in water. Although water that was shown negative words created ugly and asymmetrical crystals, water that was shown positive words created beautiful crystals. Water shown the words "Love and Gratitude," produced the most beautiful crystals.

Astonishingly, even polluted water drawn from sources that formed ugly, misshapen crystals, could be transformed and could create perfectly formed crystals after being exposed to words of love and gratitude.

The adult human body is approximately 70 per cent water. People conclude that if thoughts and words can make impressions on water, and we are made up of water, then thoughts and words can also make impressions on us.

This is another reminder about the Power of our Words as discussed throughout this book. Let's remember to choose our words wisely because they might have tangible results.

After my friend read one of Emoto's books, she wrote a note expressing love and gratitude for everything in her refrigerator. She sees it every time she opens the door, and is reminded to express gratitude for her food and drink.

In my home, I wrote a note expressing love and gratitude for the water so that I see it above my sink every time I get a glass of water to drink. I swear that the times I remember to express love and gratitude to the water, the water tastes better and sweeter. Test it out for yourself and check whether you notice a difference in the taste of your water. Emoto's books explain how we can drink this transformed water and improve our health.

When I saw Masaru Emoto at a book signing, someone asked how long it takes to express love and gratitude into the water. He responded that it happens instantly. Likewise, I spend less than a minute expressing this intention into my glass of water and notice the results.

This immediate nature of love and gratitude is helpful to keep in mind as we practice with the Power of Gratitude in the next section. The Power of Love can be expressed in an instance.

The Flip Side

In Chapter 6, we switched our trains of thought to produce good feelings instead of bad feelings. In a similar way, we can use gratitude to attract more of what we want in our lives. Using the Flip Side Technique, we use gratitude to examine what is occurring from another perspective.

We can use the same process we followed with the Mind Keys. Just as we drove our trains to different tracks to feel better, we can use the Flip Side to express gratitude for anything related to a person or situation.

When I find that I am ready to complain or condemn someone, I can take a moment to examine the Flip Side with gratitude instead. This technique is as quick and easy as thinking a single, grateful thought.

For example, "I hate my job," can be transformed into "I am grateful to have a job that pays me for my work," using the Flip Side. Or, if Penny is complaining that her spouse is constantly late, she can use the Flip Side to remind herself of something positive about her husband for which she is grateful. She will be surprised how repeating this process will transform her relationship with him.

The next time that something happens to you that you might normally complain about, stop and examine the Flip Side with gratitude. How can you transform this into a gift? How can you feel grateful in this moment in spite of, or because of what happened?

Practice using the Flip Side and you will notice that your mind becomes accustomed to approaching life from the gracious point of view, instead of a negative point of view. As we learned in the previous chapter, the emotions follow the mind, like the caboose follows the engine, and we feel good.

In addition, when we express continued gratitude we attract into our lives additional reasons to be grateful. Like Attracts Like, after all. The next technique helps us to practice that, too.

Technique 3 – Expressing Gratitude

Purpose: To attract good situations and people into your life using the Power of Gratitude.

1) Do the Calming Technique presented in the first chapter.
2) Think about at least 5 things in your life for which you are grateful. They can be people, experiences, pets, your strengths or something else.
3) Express gratitude for each of these.

This technique can be as long as you like or as short as 10 seconds. Tailor it to make it work with your beliefs. Once you have felt thankful about each of the five, then you are finished for the day. I like to do this at least once per day.

When you begin to do this on a daily basis, you may be surprised at the results. You will naturally feel more gratitude during your everyday life. In addition, you will attract more experiences and people into your life for which to be grateful.

Advanced Gratitude

At the advanced level, we express gratitude for what we truly want, even when we do not have it yet. It is taking the Power of Intention to another level. The three important keys are to believe that it is true, feel that it is true, and say that it is true.

The first key is to believe it to be true. Using a job I dislike as an example, I can say, "I am so grateful to have a job that I love." Yes, even if it is not true, I draw upon the power of the imagination to believe that it is true. We need to convince ourselves that it can and will be true for us. Once we see it in our minds and hear it in our heads, we will see it and hear it in the world.

The second key is to feel that it is true. Remember that the thoughts and emotions are joined in the train of thought. Therefore, in addition to focusing our mind energy by using our imagination, we add the power of our emotional energy. We use the Emotional Element (from Chapter 5) and **feel** as if we already have it.

What would it feel like right now if you already had what you want to bring into your life? This is important. Feel what you would feel if you already had it. Now, double that feeling.

The third key is to say that it is true now. This means to phrase everything in the present tense instead of the future tense.

Someone who is unemployed, for example, will have better results expressing gratitude by saying, "I am so grateful to have a job that I love," rather than by saying, "I am grateful for the next job that I will find." Otherwise, the desired result continues to be projected and pushed into the future, and may never actually arrive in the present.

It is not easy to remember to use the present tense. Whenever you hear yourself using a verb to indicate future tense, simply say it again using the present tense. The mind will eventually get the hang of it.

This is more about what you say to yourself in your head, than what you say to others. We all engage in self-talk and it is important to design a simple Well-Formed Intention (also from Chapter 5) that is easy to remember. Say it to yourself several times throughout the day. Once you have repeated it enough to feel confident, practice saying it out load to yourself or others to increase the power.

One that I like is, "I am so thankful that I am finding the solution to my current health challenge." To me, "finding the solution" includes finding the answer myself, or finding the right doctor or other person to help me find the solution.

Advanced Gratitude is not easy. It definitely requires more attention, intention and imagination than gratitude for what we already have. That is one reason that it is called Advanced Gratitude. The other reason is that we are expressing gratitude In Advance of receiving the result. Influencing the future is true power.

Continue to express Advanced Gratitude by believing that it is true, feeling that it is true, and saying that it is true, and one of two things will happen. In the job example, either I will find a completely new job that I love, or something will change so that I discover that now I **do** love my job. It has worked for me, and it can work for you, too.

Self Gratitude

As Masaru Emoto demonstrated, both love and gratitude are important. It is one thing to express this to other people, and it is just as important to express love and gratitude to ourselves.

Feeling powerful comes from the inside. Expressing love and gratitude for ourselves builds a strong inner foundation. This inner strength provides the space we need to create powerful intentions and actions in the world.

If we do not feel that we are worthy or that we deserve to have good people and good things in life, then we could end up sabotaging our own efforts without knowing it. If we do not think that we deserve good fortune, then we will not attract good fortune. Therefore, the rest of this chapter concentrates on experiencing and expressing Self Gratitude.

Many of us were raised to believe that our needs are not as important as the needs of others. It is crucial that each of us realizes that our needs are of the uppermost importance to our lives and the lives of people around us. Especially if other people depend on us, such as our children, a spouse, friends or someone else, it is in their best interests, too, that we continue to love ourselves and take good care of ourselves.

We need to give our bodies, souls and minds whatever they need to function most effectively. Be good to yourself, both for your benefit and for the benefit of your loved ones. Give to yourself and then you can continue to give to them.

It is like we have a gas tank full of love. As we keep giving love away to other people, we burn gas. We need to remember to routinely fill-up our own gas tank full of love and gratitude for ourselves, before we burn off too much energy for the people we love. If we do not express love and gratitude to ourselves, we run out of gas and have no more to give to other people.

There are many ways to demonstrate Self Gratitude. How many can you think of right now? Doing one thing that you listed on your Power List or Joyful List every day is a great start.

Accepting a compliment well is another way. How do you react when someone gives you unexpected praise? People who smile and say "thank you" are demonstrating Self Gratitude. Those who deny the compliment or argue about it are displaying a lack of Self Gratitude.

There is no one in the world like you. Just like each snowflake is different, you are the only one like you. Revel in your uniqueness. Discover your strengths and share them with others. Accept yourself completely.

> "Respect your efforts, respect yourself.
> Self-respect leads to self-discipline.
> When you have both firmly under your belt,
> that's real power."
> - Clint Eastwood

Technique 4 – Exploring Self Gratitude

Purpose: To learn what perfect Self Gratitude would be like.

1) Do the Calming Technique from Chapter 1.
2) Write out the phrase below and finish the sentence.
3) Repeat 19 more times (write out the phrase and finish the sentence) so that you write down the first 20 things that come to your mind in less than five minutes. Be impulsive, and write anything down that comes into your head, even if it does not seem to make sense.

If I loved myself completely, I would

_____

Now you know some of the ideas that you have about loving yourself. Are you surprised by any of them? Use these as clues for where you can start to practice Self-Gratitude.

I love to show myself that I love myself more than anyone else in the world. It is so freeing to do all the things for myself that I have wanted others to do for me. I can buy my own flowers and massages for myself whenever I want them. I do not have to wait until Valentine's Day and hope that someone else will know what I want and buy that for me. These are examples of caring for myself, which is addressed in the next section.

Self Care

Self Care is a big component of Self Gratitude. It is important that we each take care of ourselves like our most beloved friend or family member. This means taking care of all of our needs at every level.

We all have a variety of needs. These include spiritual needs, emotional needs, intellectual needs, social needs and the body has very physical needs. No one else can take better care of ourselves than we can, because we know what we need and when we need it. If we wait for someone else to notice and give us what we need, we could be waiting a very long time.

Although all of our needs are equally important, the body's needs may be most important. If we are not feeling physically good, it is hard to feel mentally, emotionally or spiritually good.

For example, if I do not get enough sleep, my body feels terrible, my eyes hurt and I have no energy. This lack of tending to my physical needs affects me mentally and emotionally. As a result, I cannot think straight, and I have a tendency to feel hopeless and depressed.

I have known people who drive their bodies like they are slaves. These people are often surprised that they are sick a lot of the time. I believe that their bodies are making attempts to communicate with them.

I know other people who listen to their bodies and treat them as well as they can by getting good sleep and good nutrition. It is not an accident that these people often tend to look younger than they are.

Our bodies need to last throughout our entire lifetimes. As we age, we come to realize that the physical body is more fragile than we thought. Staying up all night is no longer as easy and fun as it used to be.

I have made a conscious effort to be gentler with my body. For example, I drink filtered water as often as I can. I notice that I feel better after I eat certain foods, so I eat those and avoid others that make me feel badly later. Although I dislike the extra time that it takes to stretch out before and after my exercise routine, I notice that I am less likely to pull a muscle, so I do it.

In *Women Who Run with the Wolves*, Dr Estes explains about the true nature of the body.

"...body is understood
as a being in its own right,
one who loves us, depends on us,
one to whom we are sometimes mother,
and who sometimes is mother to us."
- Dr. Clarissa Pinkola Estes

When the body's needs are addressed, we feel strong enough to move on to address our other needs. Feeling physically good provides the capacity to do the Mind Keys and other techniques that care for our emotional needs. It also gives us the energy to care for other people.

Our spiritual needs also have to be met for us to feel as powerful as we truly are. Of course, that means different things to different people. It also might mean different things at various times in our lives. What we need to do to meet our needs today may be completely different from what we needed 10 years ago, or from what we may need 10 years from now. The point is to listen to what our souls need and to meet those needs.

We may also have intellectual needs and social needs. What other needs do you have?

When we feel that all of our needs are met, we glory in our Power and other people notice. Remember that you are a role model to others. As your children, friends and other loved ones watch and listen to you taking good care of yourself, they learn that they have the freedom to do that, too. Be a great role model and demonstrate to others how to remain powerful at work and at home so that they can learn how to do that, too.

To summarize this chapter, we can express the Power of Love in our lives in an instant by Redirecting Energy to transform any situation. Love and gratitude can transform our lives when we use it with others and when we express love and gratitude towards ourselves, and towards our bodies, minds, and souls.

Conclusion

This book has covered a wide range of areas and examples to help us to Choose Power in our everyday lives. We now have a collection of tools and techniques that we can use at home and work.

We have learned different ways to feel powerful in our bodies. We know words and skills that help us to have Power with People. In addition to knowing how to improve communication with others, we know how to limit and end relationships when necessary.

We used the Power in our Body to move pendulums. We have learned how the Power of Intention takes the Power of Attraction to the next level. We can drive our trains of thought so that we are more in control of our minds and emotions. Finally, we can use the Power of Love and Self Gratitude to enhance our lives.

How will you know when it is time to use a tool or technique? Perhaps every time that you notice a cloud, you will be reminded about the shifting nature of emotions, and to use the Mind Keys. Maybe the next time that you are "on automatic" washing dishes or doing something similar you will remember to think about what you really want in your life, as you figured out in the My Ideal Life Technique.

Practice the Calming Technique at a long stoplight (keeping your eyes open). When you find yourself starting to complain about someone or something, use gratitude to examine the Flip Side.

There are many opportunities to practice and use these techniques. Specific techniques may speak to you today, while others may call out to you in a month or two.

Mixing and Matching

The tools and techniques can also be mixed and matched. I bet that some of you have already started to do that. For example, the Power Pose works very well with the Calming Technique. Take a Power Bath while you do the Pet Peeve technique. In the middle of a difficult technique like Releasing Heavy Heart Energy, do the Power Pose.

Play and have fun with the different techniques. Intentional Meditation in Appendix A also offers additional ways to put the techniques together.

Life is made up of good and bad experiences. No one can escape having bad things happen to them. My book has discussed some experiences that are not often discussed with others, such as the need to grieve, and how to handle a stalker. Because our society splits the good off from the bad, sometimes it is easier to ignore the bad and pretend that bad things do not happen.

The truth is that each and every person experiences "bad" things in life. Deep down we know this to be true. We all have challenges, and hard times and endings in life.

We all have had a "bad day," when everything seems to go wrong, and it is important to know that we are not being punished when this seems to happen. It is a fact of life that there are good days and there are bad days. The point is to enjoy our lives and feel good as often as we can, in spite of the trials and tribulations. Just because one thing goes wrong, we do not have to expect to have a "bad day." Our luck can change at any time.

In addition, have you noticed that the "bad things" that happen in our lives often bring unexpected blessings? For example, I was devastated when I was laid off from a job in the 1990's. However, my next employer hired me at a 60 per cent higher salary than the previous job. Also, I needed to endure a very painful break-up so that I could Creatively Visualize the perfect partner for me, and then let him find me. Therefore, we can redefine those bad things as learning experiences or personal growth opportunities.

Remember to use the Mind Keys to get back on track and feel

better as soon as possible. Feeling badly is just a reminder. Just like a fever can tell us that we are not in good health, we can take our emotional temperature to check in with ourselves, and then let bad feelings go. We can still feel good and powerful in spite of what happens.

Those of you who are jumping around in this book still have surprises in store. When you have read it all, you are ready to pull out your favorite techniques. Some of them are good to do on a daily basis, such as the Calming Technique, the Power Pose, and Expressing Gratitude.

Once in a while, you might choose a sampling of techniques to do together, like choosing recipes for a special seven course meal. Mix in your favorite ingredients.

Pampering is important, and this is one great way to pamper ourselves. Both men and women need to take time for ourselves to process the events in our lives and grow into stronger, healthier adults who choose to live powerfully and inspire others to do the same.

Here is a sample menu. Or, create your own concoction.

Sample Seven-Course Meal

Choose some time that you have all to yourself.
1) Start or finish with a Power Bath, whichever you prefer.
2) Sit comfortably and do the Calming Technique.
3) Do the Power Pose.
4) State a Well-Formed Intention for this session.
5) Do one or more of the following techniques:
   Creative Visualization
   Releasing Heavy Heart Energy
   Transforming a Negative Emotion
   My Ideal Life
   Create a Power List
   Design a Joyful List

Practice with the pendulum techniques

Any technique from Chapter 7

Or, simply practice Slowing Down Time.

6) Spend a moment doing the White Light Technique for each loved one.

7) Finish up by Expressing Gratitude.

We are all on journeys throughout our lives. We meet a range of people along the way, experience unforgettable adventures and ride emotional roller-coasters. This is inevitable. Now we know how to enjoy the journey more by rejuvenating our bodies, dealing with people effectively and attracting more of what we truly want into our lives so that we feel more love and gratitude.

I wish you, the reader, the very best of luck, the gentlest learning experiences and the most personal power on your journey through life. I am honored that you have chosen this book. I express love and gratitude for the loved ones you tell about this book so that all of us can experience truly powerful lives. We can all enjoy our journeys more of the time and more deeply now as we Choose Power.

"This life is yours.
Take the power to choose what you want to do and do it well.
Take the power to love what you want in life and love it honestly.
Take the power to walk in the forest and be a part of nature.
Take the power to control your own life.
No one else can do it for you.
Take the power to make your life happy."
- Susan Polis Schutz

Appendix A

This is a supplement to the Calming Technique that is taught in Chapter 1. Additional recommendations are provided here for those of you who want to learn more.

Meditation Basics

Different types of meditation exist, such as walking, chanting and dance meditation; plus, a tremendous variety of meditation techniques are available. Therefore, it is important to say that there is no wrong way to meditate. Some people prefer to meditate in the morning; some prefer to meditate in the evening. If you already have a routine that works for you, I encourage you to continue with your practice.

Meditation increases our sense of power in everyday life. Not only does the mind and body experience noticeable positive effects both during and immediately after meditation, these positive effects naturally generalize to other areas of our lives. During times when I am not even thinking about meditating, I realize that I can choose my emotional state. For example, I notice that I could easily get angry in a specific situation, and now I can let it go and experience fewer intense feelings.

Follow up with any person, book or event that crosses your path regarding meditation. As discussed in Chapter 4, we naturally attract into our lives the experiences and information which we need when we need them.

Recommendations

The following three recommendations can help you to begin or to improve your meditation practice. These include meditating in the same place and at the same time, gradually increasing the length of your sessions and using a mantra. After that, Intentional Meditation ends this section.

My first recommendation is to meditate in the same place every time that you do it, if you can. Ideally, this place would be different from the places where you watch television, read or sleep. This is important in the beginning because it teaches your mind to associate sitting in this place with the relaxed, meditative mind state. Thus, your mind and body become conditioned, and it becomes easier for you to get into that meditative mind state whenever you sit in that same place.

Meditating at the same time each day is also helpful to teach the brain to meditate. Some people love to meditate first thing in the morning. I love to meditate every night before I go to bed. Meditating in the evening calms my mind so I can let go of the day's happenings and my current worries, and I have an easier time getting to sleep. Everyone is different; so do what works well for you.

My second recommendation is to gradually increase the length of your meditation sessions. Although you might start out with 5 -10 minute sessions, as you experience the renewed calm, peace and power, you might find yourself naturally extending your meditation sessions to 20 or 30 minutes, or even longer. Of course, time is an issue in a busy life, so do what works best for you. Continue to treat your meditation session like a gift to yourself.

My third recommendation is to experiment with using a mantra to occupy your mind and help to keep it quiet. A mantra is a word or phrase that may have personal or spiritual meaning for you, or it might just be something you give your mind to "chew" on because it is used to being busy. This is especially helpful when you are beginning to meditate and your mind is not yet used to being quiet.

Keeping the mind busy with a mantra keeps it from bringing other thoughts into your mind, as it has a habit of doing. Other thoughts, such as upcoming tasks or events, or relationship issues may take your mind's energy away from your focus. When it happens, that is okay. Return your mind's focus to the mantra whenever you notice other thoughts entering your mind.

Here are some ideas that you might use for a mantra. Notice that they are all pretty simple. You might choose another positive word that you prefer. Perhaps you want to experiment with different words in order to discover what works best for you. Or, you might choose to stick with one.

I like to concentrate on the word slowly with every breath in and every breath out. Some people mix and match so that they concentrate on one word when they breathe in and another word when they breathe out. For example, use "Breathe" on the in-breath and "Clear" on the out-breath.

One	Reminds us that everyone and everything is connected.
Om	Used traditionally in Eastern traditions.
Clear	Reminds us to clear the mind.
Breathe	Reminds us to breathe regularly and deeply when meditating.
Love	Evokes good feelings.

Whenever you notice your mind drifting and following other thoughts, return your mind to the mantra. Simply let the thoughts go when you notice your mind has grasped on to something. Continue to return your mind to the mantra with the intention of clearing your mind.

Eventually, your mind will learn how to float free of thoughts for extended periods of time. This is when you may start to experience those moments of true bliss (discussed in Chapter 1) and you will agree that meditation is a true gift to yourself.

Meditating with a Group

Many people report benefits from meditating with a group. You might explore this with a local group to check whether this works for you.

On the plus side, you might find that you experience the deep, meditative state more quickly and more deeply than when meditating alone. Having a group of people around you in that meditative mind state will naturally draw your mind into the same state. On the minus side, I have noticed that I am easily distracted by other people's movements and noises, so I do group meditation on a limited basis.

I do enjoy meditating with my partner on a regular basis. We do this together just before we go to sleep. I feel more connected to my partner because of this practice. It is amazing how often we are on the "same page" and can almost read each other's minds, and I believe this is because we meditate together.

Intentional Meditation

The first goal of meditation is to be able to clear the mind whenever we choose. This can help us to calm the mind, decrease anxiety, relax the circulatory system and overcome insomnia, among other results.

Once we have learned to clear the mind at will, then we can use our mind as a sharp, focused tool to launch an intention. The examples below provide some possible places to start. Experiment with one of the following, or create your own intentions:

~ Send out healing, loving energy to your friends and family. Focus on each person for a short period of time and ask that they be kept "healthy and strong" or whatever blessings or positive intentions you want to send them. Or, if you prefer to send loving energy to one particular person, then focus the entire energy from one meditative session towards that one person.

~ Practice Creative Visualization and picture future events that you want to occur. Be as specific as you can be. What does it look like? What does it sound like? What does it feel like? (Chapter 5 addresses Creative Visualization in more detail.)

~ If you have a question or are "stuck" about a particular personal problem or situation, you can ask for a solution. Once you have entered the still, meditative state, then ask your question. Clear your mind again so that it is open and receptive to the ideas that will bloom. I have experienced tremendous insights and answers about my body, my work situations and other areas of my life by doing this.

~ In the middle of your meditation, practice the Power Pose, presented in Chapter 1. Notice how it increases your energy and focus. After 20 seconds or three deep breaths, bring your hands and arms down and return to the meditation alone. Notice that you can add the Power Pose to your meditation whenever you choose to increase your power.

Undoubtedly, meditation can increase positive effects within the body, mind and spirit. As you continue to practice, you can experience amazing outcomes beyond your wildest dreams. Enjoy your journey on this inner road.

Appendix B

Power from Fire

Some people feel restored by fire, while others do not. If you regularly burn a lot of candles, or have a fireplace where you enjoy building fires, then you are likely to be one of those who restore their power with fire.

If you do not know, or if you are not sure, then experiment with candles. When the lights are replaced with candlelight, does it add to your energy or decrease your feelings of power? Or, does it not seem to have an effect on you one way or the other?

Another way to use the Power from Fire is to burn sage. It helps negative emotions and other bad energy to "go up in smoke." We are often left feeling refreshed, like we have just awakened from a nap. Burning sage in an area where there has been disagreements will clear out that negative energy so that people can come back to the area with fresh viewpoints and no longer feel the negative energy in the area.

The purpose of the next technique is to use fire to recharge yourself and to cleanse your environment. If this is new to you, think about how you may have smelled incense or frankincense or myrrh burning in your church. This is very similar.

Technique – Smudging

Purpose: To use fire to clear out bad energy.

Sage can be purchased from a variety of stores, such as New Age and Native American ones, and it is sold in different ways. The sage may be sold as leaves alone, or as stems with the leaves still on them, or as bundles of the stems.

Make sure you have something safe to burn the sage in. Abalone shells (or conch shells) work well to contain the burning sage, and are usually sold in the same places where you purchase sage. You might have something else that would work well, like an ashtray, or a ceramic bowl. All dishes can get hot, so be careful when working with fire.

The two techniques below contain steps to use sage to cleanse yourself and to cleanse your environment. Do the first technique when you are feeling tired or confused, and want to feel more powerful. I like to do it when I am feeling angry or depressed, because burning sage helps to clear out negative energy and bad feelings. Do the second one when you want to cleanse an area, such as when you move into a new home, or before using a space for an important event.

Steps to empower yourself with sage
1) Sit comfortably.
2) Use matches or a lighter to light some sage in an appropriate container. Immediately blow out the flames so the sage continues to smoke.
3) Circle the sage around your face and around your body. The smoke and smell of sage calms many people down and reduces anxiety.

Steps to cleanse out an area
1) Use matches or a lighter to light some sage in an appropriate container. Immediately blow out the flames so the sage continues to smoke throughout the following steps. Repeat by lighting more sage if the leaves stop smoking.
2) Carry the container of burning sage as you walk around

the inside of your home. Walk along every wall as you trace your way along the entire inside perimeter of your home.

3) When you get to each door and each window that could be used as an entrance, stop and circle the sage with your arm three times. Send out an intention that only people with good intentions are allowed to cross this threshold. Come back to your starting point to complete the circle.

If the sage begins to smoke a lot, then there may be bad energy, so take more time to let the sage burn in that area. Also, spend time letting it burn above the bed. Continue to move the sage in circles above your bed, so that every square inch comes in contact with the smoke.

My mother believes that burning sage the night before her events cleanses the buildings of negative energy and encourages people to spend money more freely. For example, vendors make better money.

I also used to work for a company that believed in the benefits of sage. The CEO of the company had noticed that it helped to produce better results when burned the night before big sales meetings. As a result, it became a tradition throughout different offices in the company, and the company also began selling it along with the shells to burn it in.

As with all of the tools and techniques in this book, I recommend testing them out to decide how well they work for you. We are in a state of constant change, so respect and listen to the changing needs of our bodies, minds and spirits. They all help us to know intuitively what we need and what is best for us.

References

Byrne, R. (2006). *The Secret.* New York: Simon & Schuster, Inc.

Chopra, Deepak. (1994). *The Seven Spiritual Laws of Success.* California: New World Library.

Covey, Stephen. R. (1989). *The Seven Habits of Highly Effective People: Powerful Lessons in Personal Change.* New York: Simon & Schuster, Inc. Quote from page 109.

Cousins, Norman. (1979). *Anatomy of an Illness as Perceived by the Patient.* New York: Bantam Books.

de Becker, G. (1997). *The Gift of Fear: Survival Signals that Protect Us from Violence.* USA: Little, Brown and Company.

Emoto, M. (2003). *The True Power of Water.* Oregon: Beyond Words Publishing, Inc.

Estes, Clarissa. P. (1992). *Women Who Run with the Wolves.* New York: Ballantine Books. Quote from page 208.

Frankl, Victor. E. (1984). *Man's Search for Meaning.* New York: Simon & Schuster, Inc.

Selected Index

BOOKS

O is a symbol of the world, of oneness and unity. In different cultures it also means the "eye", symbolizing knowledge and insight. We aim to publish books that are accessible, constructive and that challenge accepted opinion, both that of academia and the "moral majority".

Our books are available in all good English language bookstores worldwide. If you don't see the book on the shelves ask the bookstore to order it for you, quoting the ISBN number and title. Alternatively you can order online (all major online retail sites carry our titles) or contact the distributor in the relevant country, listed on the copyright page.

See our website www.o-books.net for a full list of over 400 titles, growing by 100 a year.

And tune in to myspiritradio.com for our book review radio show, hosted by June-Elleni Laine, where you can listen to the authors discussing their books.

MySpiritRadio